GROW YOUR OWN

BOTANICALS

DELICIOUSLY
PRODUCTIVE
PLANTS FOR
HOMEMADE DRINKS,
REMEDIES AND
SKINCARE

CINEAD McTERNAN

PHOTOGRAPHY BY TORY McTERNAN

FOR HAL, FROM CINEAD
FOR AVA, GEROGE & PAUL,
FROM TORY

DISCLAIMER: The information in this book is for
educational purposes, to inform the reader. It is not a
replacement for professional medical advice and
treatment. Neither the author nor the publisher can
be held responsible for any adverse reactions to the
recipes, recommendations and instructions contained
herein, and the use of any herb or derivative is entirely
at the reader's own risk.

An Hachette UK Company
www.hachette.co.uk

First published in Great Britain in 2019 by
Kyle Books, an imprint of Kyle Cathie Ltd
Carmelite House
50 Victoria Embankment
London EC4Y 0DZ
www.kylebooks.co.uk

Distributed in the US by Hachette Book Group, 1290
Avenue of the Americas, 4th and 5th Floors, New
York, NY 10104.

Distributed in Canada by Canadian Manda Group,
664 Annette St., Toronto, Ontario, Canada M6S 2C8.

ISBN: 978 085783 531 4

10 9 8 7 6 5 4 3 2 1

Photographer: Tory McTernan
Illustrator: Aaron Blecha
Design: Nicky Collings
Project Editor: Sophie Allen
Editorial assistant: Isabel Gonzalez-Prendergast
Production: Lucy Carter

A Cataloguing in Publication record for this title is
available from the British Library.

Printed and bound in China

CONTENTS

INTRODUCTION

As I write this, it's mid-June and I'm staying with my sister (the photographer of this book) in Somerset, England. I've just taken her two children and my son to the local market town for ice cream, which actually turned out to be gelato. (My son wants me to add that the shop was Ecco Gelato in Sherbourne. He loves it and thinks they'd love to have the namecheck.) Among the usual flavours, I was excited to see a gelato made from sea buckthorn berries. If I am being picky, it's not the season for the berries, but then again, would I feel like eating gelato in October? Either way, the gelato was a beautiful shade of orange and tasted delicious – a delicate, slightly sour flavour with a fresh, faintly floral finish that reminded my niece of cola cubes.

Sea buckthorn grows naturally in hedgerows and inhospitable-looking sand dunes. If you enjoy blustery coastal walks around the UK, the chances are you'll probably have spotted the prickly shrubs along your travels, especially in the autumn, when they're laden with clusters of gorgeously vibrant fruits, which are very high in both vitamins and antioxidants. The fact that sea buckthorn features on the menu of the little gelato parlour has made my day because it's one of the botanicals I'm growing for this book (see page 74). Clearly there's an appetite for interesting flavours derived from edible plants, and it's not just confined to fancy metropolitan folk.

I experienced a similar sense of excitement filming for BBC *Gardeners' World* at a recent RHS Flower Show. Specialist nurseries were showcasing the kind of plants that nowadays we use to brighten up containers or borders but were traditionally grown for the kitchen or medicine cabinet. The rather shaggy but heavenly clove-scented carnation (or pink) 'Mrs Sinkins' was particularly eye-catching. During the Victorian era this annual was commonly used as an edible decoration for food or to flavour soups and sauces. I had a lengthy chat with the nurseryman and we came up with all manner of ways to make the most of the petals of this unkempt little flower, including syrups, mulled wine and, of course, cakes. I'd already sown seeds of its relative the clove pink (*Dianthus caryophyllus*) – see page 65 – but I couldn't resist buying this variety, too. For me, it's exactly the variety of plant to capture the imagination of the new generation of growers who are looking to experiment with what they choose to grow. It's cheap, easily raised from seed and doesn't need acres of land to produce a harvest.

REDISCOVERING EDIBLE PLANTS

If we look back at our rich horticultural heritage, we have a wealth of knowledge about useful plants; we just need to rediscover it. According to the Chelsea Physic Garden's website, of the "more than 20,000 different edible plants on Earth, only around 20 are in common production". I recommend visiting the Chelsea Physic Garden in London; it's an inspiring place to visit and a fantastic jumping-off point for those of us who would like to grow something a bit more interesting and, when space and time is at a premium, useful.

With the global population set to reach 8.6 billion by 2030, looking to our own backyards to create wildlife habitats, promote better mental health from beautiful green surroundings and, of course, produce delicious homegrown food and drink is surely taking a small but important step in the right direction. In a time when we're overwhelmed by technology, struggle to manage the waste we create and are thoughtlessly harming our environment, growing stuff seems a simple and sensible contribution we can make towards a better world. And it's fun, rewarding and healthy, too.

Thanks to horticulturists like Jekka McVicar (who knew she was on to something over 30 years ago when she started her organic nursery – and has been the leading herb expert ever since) and the science-loving, green-fingered guru James Wong (who coined the concept of horticultural geek chic), as well as inspiring growers like Alys Fowler and Mark Diacono, an increasing number of us aren't content with buying bland bedding plants from the local DIY store to fill a few plastic window boxes. Instead, we're discovering that, with a little extra research and thought, our growing experience can be elevated to raising homegrown plants with a bewildering array of uses that go far beyond simply providing a tonic to quell a queasy tummy (though never underestimate the benefits of peppermint and chamomile tea for aiding digestion). Today, we can grow an exciting assortment of plants that provide a fascinating and diverse bounty that can be used to make marshmallows, liquorice-flavoured sweets, herby spirits and exotically flavoured syrups.

SMALL IS BEAUTIFUL

More and more of us are taking up the challenge to fill our backyards, however tiny, with a range of plant varieties that earn their keep by providing not only pretty flowers but also tasty treats. Even if you only have a balcony or window box, you'll still have enough space to grow a few plants that provide roots, shoots, stems, leaves or flowers that can be used in some interesting and useful ways. Throughout the book, I've tried to think about how little outdoor space many of us who are interested in growing our own actually have. I often refer to my own garden as postage stamp-sized, and at 4.5 x 3m (15 x 10ft), it is small, so it comes naturally to think about growing plants in containers that can be moved to suit the occasion – or to just give me the chance to change the look of my garden at times when I'm yearning for plenty of room in which to play with plants and try things out – as well as particular plants and ways of growing them that work well when space is restricted.

THE BOTANICAL REVOLUTION

I love the word "botanical". The Oxford English Dictionary defines a botanical as "a substance obtained from a plant and used typically in medicinal or cosmetic products". Horticulturists may find my use of the word "botanical" a little woolly because some herbs are included in this book while others aren't. However, I hope that the word will seduce a new group of growers to get their fingers dirty, delight their friends with natural cocktails and revel in the wonder of watching a seed become a plant. Herb, aromatic, edible, botanical – call it what you will, please just grow it.

HOW TO USE THIS BOOK

Please consider this book to be an introduction to the wonderful world of useful plants. I've included growing advice and care tips, as well as some suggestions on how to make the most of your harvest, but this information is not exhaustive.

While researching this book, I was frequently surprised to discover that plants that I thought had no use beyond their pretty blooms could, in fact, be dried to make a tea or infused to flavour a vinegar. I was inspired to get into my kitchen, not just to chop up freshly picked herbs to add to a salad, delicious as that is, but to revel in the flamboyance and generosity of botanicals. Whether I was creating a decadent syrup to flavour a cocktail to share with my friends or making a face cream to give as a gift, filling my own small plot with useful plants became both thrilling and addictive in equal measure.

Choosing plants is always the most exciting part of any new project – it's the dreaming stage. Initially, the list of plants I wanted to include in this book ran to the hundreds; a brain dump of plant names that I wasn't sure it was even possible to grow in my small garden in the UK. Eventually, I realized that this long list had to be pared down to a realistic number that would help you, the reader, create a beautiful garden. So, after greedily poring over books and seed catalogues, as well as spending hours online, I decided that the best way to approach this task was to work out which of the many benefits of growing botanicals were most appealing.

I've selected botanicals that I hope will capture your imagination, but I urge you to be curious, too. I recommend reading about the plants you already love or have bought spontaneously because you might be surprised to discover their remedial and kitchen benefits. I've created a collection of plants that are a great starting point, with easy-to-grow varieties that offer long seasons of interest, as well as more tender or unusual varieties that require a little more in the way of TLC to reap their benefits.

The book is arranged in two parts. The first part provides you with some basic information about growing plants. Whether you're planting in a border or container, you'll learn all you need to know to get you off to a flying start. Rather than repeating the same instructions in each botanical entry, I've put all the general advice for harvesting and drying plants at the front of the book.

The second part of the book presents the botanicals. It's a quick guide to growing, caring for and using your plants. I've tried to focus on need-to-know information, though the temptation to digress and include lots of other details was hard to resist. I want this book to be a useful reference that you can quickly consult as you're planting or picking. I've included a few planting projects that are fun or interesting to try, as well as those that demonstrate good horticultural practice. You'll also find special features that provide you with advice for using the plants you grow, including how to make tisanes (see page 36), tinctures (see page 43), flavoured booze (see page 40) and beauty products (see page 44).

While I've recommended recipes and medicinal remedies, these suggestions are by no means comprehensive. I've tried to pick examples that are either fun, surprising or useful as a culinary or medicinal staple. Many of the plants in this book are claimed to help with more serious health problems. I am not a herbalist so you must undertake your own research if you feel you'd like to find out more about the properties of an individual plant. There are many expert publications and websites you can consult, and I've put together a reading list at the back of this book as a helpful starting point.

I hope this book will inspire you to see the world of plants from a new perspective.

TIPS FOR GROWING PLANTS
IN A SMALL GARDEN

I like to roll with the idea that the best things come in small packages. However, small can also be frustrating if you've got the gardening bug and want to be able to grow an array of blooms. Thankfully, there are some tricks you can use to be creative and make the most of your space.

The key thing about a small garden is that it won't have the breadth of aspect for you to grow a huge range of plants. It'll either be shady with a small corner that's sunny, or vice versa. For a roof garden, you'll need to consider plants that aren't bothered by exposed sites. And if you have a courtyard garden, shade-loving plants will be your go-to group. Once you know what type of environment you have, you can narrow down the field of choice, which is a good thing when space is restricted.

Think carefully about your boundaries. One option is to "borrow" your neighbour's landscape. I have two juneberry trees in my backyard and my next-door neighbours on the right-hand side have one too, so in a sense we both have three trees. We bought and planted them together to try to mask a house at the rear of our plots and to create a sense of unity along the back wall. It's a very effective technique and I really enjoyed having a chat with my neighbours over a glass of wine to pick out which trees to go for. The other trick with boundary walls and fences is to use them to grow plants vertically. I like to use climbers to grow up walls and create a lovely green effect. Varying the heights and sizes of containers – I'm thinking medium and large containers here – also helps create an interesting rhythm along a wall or fence.

Remember to restrict your colour palette and choice of plants to avoid the feeling of chaos or confusion that comes with an eclectic collection – unless, of course, that's your thing, in which case rules are

made to be broken. However, if you decide on a limited colour scheme (yellow, orange and red, for example), you mustn't be despondent when you have to pass over gorgeous blooms in other colours. Careful consideration and cohesive thinking really does work wonders. More often than not, I tend to flout this rule, believing that it is more important to grow what you love rather than what you should have. This year, I'm utterly delighted with a colour palette of white, blue and purple with the occasional pop of orange. The whole effect has tied the garden together, unlike the haphazard collection of colours seen in previous years.

Restricting your colour palette also applies to textures and shapes. Repeating plants with similar attributes is an easy way to create rhythm in a border or series of containers that helps the eye take in and "read" the entire plot.

Planting a small tree – or as many as you dare – in a tiny plot is a surprisingly counterintuitive way to make a space feel bigger. Strangely, the scale helps play with the sense of space, expanding it vertically and horizontally, encouraging your eye to look up and out across the garden. The standard, or lollipop, tree keeps a larger specimen contained. However, multi-stemmed trees can be used just as effectively, if not quite as liberally. In my opinion, trees are an overlooked asset of the small city garden, encouraging a variety of wildlife to take up residence and add to the ecosystem.

Finally, one more trick is to work with objects of different sizes to manipulate the sense of perspective in a tiny space. The idea is simple: place the largest containers and features closest to the house and then gradually reduce the scale of garden objects as you move further away from the house to accentuate the sense of perspective.

PREPARING YOUR PLOT

Whether you have a selection of small containers on a balcony, a courtyard garden or a few raised beds and borders to play with, thinking about how you're going to garden is essential before you dig your first hole or sow your first seed.

I'll wager that the very fact that you're reading this book (and by the way, thank you so much for doing so) means that you have a sense of caring for the environment and value Mother Nature. I think it's safe to assume that sprays and chemicals for controlling your plot aren't items you'll be making room for on your garden shelf. After all, you're going to be growing plants that you'll be consuming in some way or another: as a delicious drink, an addition to a meal or as a soothing face cream, for example. As this is the case, you'll need to rely on your soil to provide a foundation for your plants.

As Jekka McVicar so eloquently explains, the soil is the engine of your plot. So, feed your soil and it will nourish your plants. Choose the best soil you can. There's a great variety of peat-free, organic composts available. Yes, they are more expensive, but it's worth the initial outlay for the health, vitality and productivity of your plants. For the last few years, I've been using a biochar-based compost. It's an interesting product that helps plants establish roots quickly and introduces nutrients and microbial populations to the soil, which noticeably improves plants' health and productivity.

Soil is a fascinating subject (and it's something about which I need to learn much more). It's staggering to think that in a teaspoon of soil there are, quite literally, billions of microorganisms that play a part in the soil's lifecycle. These small living creatures, along with worms and insects, break down plant matter and animal tissue, improve soil by creating airways or introducing nutrients and

all work together to ensure plants can access air, water and nutrients. Understanding this will help you see the bigger picture, which requires us to replenish the organic matter upon which these vital microorganisms feed and thrive. I like to think it's a bit like adding water to a drink of squash: if you don't top up with some of the concentrate as well, eventually you'll be left with just a glass of water.

Mulching not only helps soil retain moisture levels and restricts weeds from growing and competing for nutrients, it also protects the top few inches of soil, which are packed to the gunnels with microorganisms, organic matter and soil nutrients.

I like to make my own fertilizers and soil improvers, growing comfrey (see page 96) to harvest the leaves and make a nutrient-rich, if somewhat smelly, liquid food that produces highly concentrated levels of nutrients that are easily absorbed by plants.

COMPOST

There are several varieties of compost to choose from:

- Peat-free compost: If you are not keen on using peat-based composts (and who can blame you, since harvesting peat from lowland bogs affects the wildlife that depends on these habitats as well as adversely affecting local ecosystems and ultimately our environment), there are plenty of alternatives on offer. In the early years of peat-free compost, it really wasn't a viable alternative as it dried out so quickly, but these days recipes and ingredients have improved and it's much more efficient. Read the label and go for a brand that provides plenty of information about how to use and care for the product. Look out for composts that have beneficial additives like biochar, seaweed and mycorrhizal fungi because these all help container-grown crops.

- Soilless compost: This type of compost can be made from a combination of materials, including peat, coir fibre, bark and vermiculite. Soilless composts are specially created for containers and particular types of plant. They offer good drainage, aeration and a neutral pH. They are also light and, generally speaking, you don't need to apply any feed for the first 6 weeks.

- Ericaceous compost: This acidic compost is ideal for crops such as blueberries and cranberries that require a soil pH value of between 4.0 and 5.0 (a neutral soil is pH 7.0; alkaline soils have a pH above 7.0). Ericaceous compost is readily available to buy from garden centres, DIY stores and online.

FREE-DRAINING COMPOST

Some crops, especially Mediterranean herbs, need a very open, free-draining growing medium. Adding horticultural grit or perlite to general composts will help provide the right conditions, by improving aeration and preventing the compost from becoming waterlogged and compacted. A good ratio to use is three parts compost to one part horticultural grit.

TIPS FOR USING COMPOST

- As a rule of thumb, one 20-litre (5-gallon) bag of compost will fill a 30cm (12in) container.

- Fill containers with compost to about 2.5cm (1in) below the rim to prevent the soil washing away over the sides when you water your plants.

- If you are completely replanting a container with new plants, it's best to use fresh compost each year. However, for large containers, remove only the top two-thirds of the compost and replace it with new compost each planting season.

- Topdressing (scraping off the top layer of old compost and refreshing with new compost) each year is sufficient for perennials that are staying in the same container until they need repotting (after 3–4 years of growth).

ALCHEMISTS OF THE SOIL

The humble earthworm is the unsung hero of the soil. Most of us are probably aware that it's a good thing if you dig a hole in your garden and see lots of worms. However, the earthworm's contribution to the health and fertility of soil is pretty incredible and goes far beyond just churning up the soil or being a bird's snack of choice. I'm not a scientist, and I don't want you to become so bored by having to wade through technical information that you find yourself wandering off to make a cup of tea, so I've kept this section brief.

In the 12 years I've worked in horticulture, I've found that the more I understand the bigger picture, the more enjoyment I derive from the subject of horticulture, and the greater the successes in my own backyard. So I hope that after reading these few paragraphs about earthworms you'll have a different view about what lies beneath, and if you do find yourself fired up by the subject, there's a list of excellent books and websites I recommend for further reading at the back of the book (see page 208).

For centuries, worms have been recognized for the vital contribution they make to the overall health and productivity of the soil. The Ancient Greek philosopher Aristotle acknowledged their importance as the "intestines of the Earth", and Ancient Egypt's Queen Cleopatra supposedly decreed earthworms to be sacred animals, forbidding Egyptian farmers to disturb or remove them from the land for fear it affected the soil's fertility. Of course, Charles Darwin sums up their importance most succinctly:

"The plough is one of the most ancient and most valuable of man's inventions; but long before he existed the land was, in fact, regularly ploughed, and still continues to be thus ploughed, by earthworms. It may be doubted whether there are many other animals which have played so important a part in the history of the world, as have these lowly organized creatures."

The key thing to know is that earthworms chomp their way through all manner of organic matter, which, once processed through their guts, is transformed into worm casts that are rich with microbial activity, have a high nutrient content and help to improve the soil's structure and water retention – all essential benefits for healthy plant growth. To my mind, it's a horticultural form of alchemy.

WORMERIES

If you don't have soil in your backyard, don't despair. You can still enjoy the benefits worms bring to the garden by setting up a wormery to keep your own pet worms. Not only will they create a perfect friable compost that's ideal for sowing seeds or potting up your plants (indoor or outdoor) and produce a liquid that's a fantastic fertilizer but they'll eat your kitchen scraps, too.

Food waste is a serious issue. Just as gardeners compost green waste, recycling uneaten food instead of throwing it away – and remember, there's no such place as "away" – will reduce the strain on landfill sites. I've only recently begun my own wormery but I highly recommend it.

Most wormeries consists of at least two compartments: a lower tray that collects liquid and an upper composting area where the kitchen waste is added and the worms actively work. It's a very simple concept and could be made by using large plastic tubs or even rubbish bins.

The idea is that you provide worms with a homely, humid layer of coir or other bedding material, where they can hide, rest up and begin to digest their food. Kitchen waste (chopped up into manageable pieces) is added on top of this layer, which encourages worms to fetch pieces and bring them down into their burrows. Once the worm compost is ready to use, add another tray on top to fill with bedding material and kitchen waste; the worms will then migrate into the new tray in order to reach the food supply, leaving behind a rich, friable soil. Worms are most active in warm, moist conditions, so find a spot for your wormery that won't get too cold in winter or too hot in summer. I store mine under the workbench in my glasshouse during the summer; the bench provides shade for the wormery and I keep the door, vents and windows of the glasshouse open to provide the right conditions for the worms.

FEEDING YOUR WORMS

Worms will enjoy the following food:

- Cooked and raw vegetables (keep onions, shallots, garlic and leeks to a minimum, but if added, preferably they should be cooked).

- Fruit, apart from citrus.

- Coffee grounds, teabags, eggshells and a little bread (think the odd crust rather than an entire slice).

- Small amounts of newspaper or plain paper (definitely not glossy magazines).

- A few handfuls of green garden waste.

Avoid adding meat, fish, bones, fat and woody plant waste to your wormery as these items will attract pests. If you find lots of flies in your wormery, cover the kitchen waste with a layer of damp newspaper or bury the kitchen waste in the compost. If your wormery becomes smelly, stop feeding the worms with kitchen waste and wait until they've had a chance to eat what's there. The compost in the wormery might be too wet, so check for excess liquid and drain off, if necessary.

THE KEY FEATURES OF A WORMERY ARE:

A bottom tray that can collect liquid. You can add a tap to this or simply tip the liquid out into another receptacle. This liquid can be used like any concentrated plant food, diluted to a ratio of one part concentrate to ten parts water.

An upper tray (or trays) with holes drilled into the bottom to allow the liquid to drain through to the bottom tray. The holes also allow the worms to move from tray to tray if you're using more than one upper tray.

A lid for the top tray to stop rain flooding the wormery and to prevent any escapees – though this shouldn't be an issue if your wormery is functioning properly and isn't too wet, smelly or suffocating for the worms.

TOOLS

You will need a few tools to help you get started and allow your botanical garden to flourish.

Hand trowels are incredibly useful. They can be used to scoop compost, dig holes for plants and remove weeds. Ergonomically designed handles are worth the extra outlay, and a stainless-steel trowel is a much better option than a plastic one as it will last longer.

A decent pair of secateurs is another must. A sharp, clean cut when you're pruning or harvesting helps to ensure that plants stay healthy.

A 10-litre (2½-gallon) watering can is a decent size for watering container-grown plants; anything smaller and you'll spend your life marching back and forth to fill it up. A watering can rose is essential for young plants and seedlings, otherwise the water will crush them. A hosepipe is also helpful when it comes to watering, unless, of course, there's a hosepipe ban. I use a retractable hose that can be conveniently stored on the tap and so doesn't take up very much space.

You might not consider labels to be tools, but actually they're one of my most important pieces of garden equipment. I used to think I'd always remember what each plant was. The garden's small, right? However, fed up of regularly forgetting the names and, more often than not, the cultivars of my plants, I've become diligent about labelling them.

A spade is helpful If you're digging in beds and borders but one certainly isn't required for container gardening. The same goes for forks, rakes and hoes. All of them are helpful if you've got a bit of space, but if your soil is contained in pots then you can happily give them a miss.

A wheelbarrow is another luxury item. It will be out of the question if you have a small backyard, though it might be worth considering buying one with some friends, especially if those friends have the room to store it, and you can borrow it as needed.

Depending on your preference, gardening gloves are either essential or a nuisance – I fall into the latter category and have the broken nails to prove it. (I love the feeling of the soil and gloves just get in the way.) There are plenty of types of gloves on offer and they are a good idea if you have sensitive skin or a job that requires you to turn up with clean fingernails.

A NOTE ABOUT WATERING

Unlike crops grown in the ground, container-grown plants cannot put down their roots to reach a natural water source. Even a good shower of rain won't always give your crops a decent drink because their leaves may be too dense to let enough water through. As a general rule, smaller pots dry out more quickly than larger ones. If in doubt, check that the compost isn't dry, and in hot weather be prepared to water once, sometimes twice, a day.

That said, overwater your plants and you'll most likely cause leaves to wilt or the plant to die. The best way to avoid this is to make sure that the pot has sufficient drainage, with holes in the bottom of the container and a layer of crocks underneath the soil. If you're unsure whether your container needs watering, check to see if the compost feels moist. If it does, there's no need to water.

A good trick to ensure that your plants receive water right where it's needed (in other words, at their roots) is to insert an upturned plastic tube (or bottle with the bottom cut off) into the soil and to fill it each time you water. This way it will deliver the water to the plant's roots as opposed to the surrounding compost. It's also worth adding a layer of mulch, such as decorative gravel, to containers to help the soil retain moisture. For borders and beds, you can use robust mulches like bark, well-rotted manure and gravel.

If you're using a watering can, take the rose off when watering beds, borders or containers in order to direct a steady flow of water to the roots rather than spraying the foliage. However, always use a rose when watering young seedlings and delicate plants to prevent them being damaged by the weight of water being poured over them.

If you are going away on holiday and can't persuade a friend to water your plants, it's worth trying either water-retaining granules, which are only a short-term solution, or a watering system that connects to your tap, which is much easier to install than you might imagine and doesn't need to cost the earth.

SOWING SEEDS

I have a bit of a love-hate relationship when it comes to sowing seeds. Well, that's not strictly true; I mostly love the job. I relish the ritual of preparing the workbench, choosing the trays or pot, tamping down the compost and watering it before I even reach for the packet of seeds. I love sprinkling the seeds and writing the label. I find all these tasks immensely satisfying. Then there's the thrill of seeing a seedling pushing through the soil, seedcase clinging on to one of the cotyledons (embryonic leaves) like a cowboy on a bucking bronco. So it's not that surprising that I find it a bit demoralizing when the seeds fail, either because the seeds themselves weren't viable or they suffered from damping off, which is the case more often than not if I've over- or underwatered them. However, this is the reality of sowing seeds. When the going's good, you can't beat it; but when it's bad, well, let's keep things in perspective, you just have to pick yourself up and try again.

Some plants featured in this book are best raised from cuttings or grown on as a small plant. However, many can be direct sown, which is good news because seeds are much cheaper than buying plug plants or plants and, as I've said, sowing seeds can be truly rewarding.

Depending on the number of seeds you are sowing, choose a 9cm (3½in) pot, a seed tray or a modular tray. Whichever type of tray or pot you use, always fill it with seed compost up to just under the rim of the tray or pot and use another pot or a "tamper" tool to tamp down the soil – you're looking to create a firm, flat surface upon which the seeds can sit. Water the compost before sowing.

Sow the seeds at the depth directed on the seed packet. It's best to sow on the surface of the compost then cover the seeds with enough compost to achieve the correct depth. To do this, make sure you leave enough room at the top of the pot or tray when you initially fill it to accommodate the extra layer of compost.

For large seeds, such as those of beans and pumpkins, use a pen or your finger to make a planting hole to the appropriate depth in the compost, drop one seed into the hole and cover with compost.

For fine seeds, sow on the surface of the compost and use a layer of vermiculite rather than compost to cover the seeds. Vermiculite is lighter than compost and it provides a bit of support as the seeds germinate and the vulnerable seedlings emerge.

The ideal place for most seeds to germinate is in a warm, dry environment such as a glasshouse or potting-shed, though a sunny windowsill will do just as well. Cover your tray or pot with a plastic bag propped up with a short cane to keep in the moisture. Some seeds may require a heat source to trigger germination, in which case use a heated propagator with a lid. Don't let the compost dry out and make sure it isn't waterlogged, because wet compost will cause the seedlings to be vulnerable to issues such as damping off.

THE FOUR Ps

While there's no particular mystery to any of these jobs, there are a few things to consider when you're tackling them to give your plants the best possible chance of success.

PRICKING OUT & POTTING ON

Once your seedlings have emerged, most types need to be individually pricked out into 7.5cm (3½in) pots or modular trays. Fill the pots or trays with homemade leaf mould, compost from your wormery or a suitable shop-bought type. Using a pencil or dibber, make a hole in the compost that will take the seedling's roots. Holding one of the leaves rather than the tender stem, which can be crushed easily, lift the seedling out of the soil (I use a pencil for this, too, pushing the tip under the roots to help carefully lever it out) and drop it into the new hole. Shake or tap the pot or use your finger to even out the compost and then water the seedling.

Potting on requires the same technique. Seedlings already in their own pots should be potted on when they need a little more space to grow.

PLUG PLANTS

Plug plants (shop-bought seedlings grown in small plugs of compost, rather than in containers) need to be potted on into 7.5cm (3½in) pots when you receive them. After they have been potted on, leave them to grow for a month or two to develop strong root systems before planting them in their final position.

growing in or the breadth of the root span for bare-root plants. Carefully remove the pot so as not to damage the root system, or spread the roots out in the base of the hole. Place the plant in the planting hole and check that the root ball is at the same level in the new hole as it was in its original tray or pot – planting too high or too deep will stress the plant. Backfill the hole with compost and firm the soil around the stem. For bare-root plants, water a little more regularly in the early days to encourage soil to fall in around the roots.

REPOTTING

Most container-grown plants will eventually outgrow their pots – the telltale sign being a mass of roots escaping from the drainage holes. You might also notice that the soil dries out quickly or, if you're able to lift the plant out of the pot, its roots are tightly packed together with little or no spare soil. This problem is easy to resolve, simply by choosing a slightly bigger pot and transplanting the plant.

If you have problems getting the plant out of its old pot, try either turning it upside down and easing it out with sharp downward jolts, or, if it's too big to handle in this way, try knocking the pot against a bench, being careful not to break the pot. For really stubborn plants, cut around the edge of the pot with a knife and pull hard – it's not ideal, but sometimes there's no other way.

Before you replant, check the roots and remove damaged or unhealthy-looking sections. Tightly-packed roots don't do their job properly, so, using secateurs or a knife, gently cut sections around the root ball and carefully open up the tangled root system with your fingers. Repot with a good soilless compost that covers the top of the root ball by about 2.5cm (1in).

PLANTING

Some plants are supplied as bare-root plants, which are at least one-year-old field-grown plants, with the bare soilless roots packed in compost or plastic. They are a cost-effective alternative to container-grown plants. The key thing to remember is that they will need a good soak before planting in order to rehydrate the roots – just think how you would feel if you'd been packaged up for a couple of days without anything to eat or drink. While the plant is soaking, have a quick look at the roots and snip off any damaged or in-turning tendrils to help your plant thrive. Whether the plant is large or small, whether you're planting in the ground or in a container, the technique is similar. Dig a planting hole that is as deep and a little wider than the pot the plant is

PLANTS FOR FREE

One of the many things I love about gardening is that everyone can enjoy the experience of growing plants. If you don't have much time, you can garden in containers or fill a plot with low-maintenance plants that best suit their specific situation. On the other hand, if you're starting to get the gardening bug and find yourself spending more and more time pottering about among the greenery, there's plenty to keep you occupied for as little or as long as you'd like.

To my mind, propagating plants (or taking cuttings) is at the top of a gardener's to-do list. It combines a bit of everything from a horticultural perspective – tools are involved (you need a sharp knife or secateurs at the very least), it's a chance to get your hands dirty, there's an immense sense of satisfaction in watching your cuttings, quite literally, take root and, of course, there's the thriftiness of the whole procedure. And who doesn't like to be a bit canny when it comes to filling a garden, balcony or windowsill with plants?

Whenever I take cuttings, I'm never entirely convinced they're going to work. The idea that you can raise several new plants from one "parent" seems too good to be true. I confess, I've had my fair share of failures, whether I've forgotten to keep the cuttings moist or inadvertently roasted them in a sunny spot. However, more often than not Mother Nature does her magical thing and I have a few more plants at the end of the season than I started out with.

When it comes to taking cuttings, there are a few rules of thumb that, if followed, will reward you richly.

SOFTWOOD CUTTINGS

Just as the name suggests, softwood cuttings are soft, young growing tips that have been snipped off the parent plant in spring and early summer. Take cuttings first thing in the morning because the plant won't have lost any moisture at this time of day, which is important because you don't want these "soft" cuttings to be droopy. Go for flower-free shoots and snip just above a bud – the section should be about 10cm (4in) long. It's a good idea to pop the cuttings into a plastic bag while you're gathering them to try to keep them as moist as possible.

The next step is to prepare the cutting, ready for planting. You're aiming for a final cutting to be 5–10cm (2–4in) long. Find the leaf joint and make a cut just below it – this is where there is a concentration of hormone, making it the place where roots will most readily form. Remove the lower leaves so that all the cutting's energy can go into creating roots rather than leaves. Pinch out the soft tip at the top and dip the base of the cutting in hormone rooting powder.

Fill a 7cm (3in) terracotta pot with compost. Using a pencil, make a hole in the compost towards the edge of the pot and pop the cutting in the hole. You should be able to fit about five cuttings around the edge of a pot. Cover the pot with a plastic bag and place it somewhere with bottom heat if possible. A windowsill is fine, though direct light can scorch the cuttings, so cover with horticultural fleece to diffuse the light. Remove the plastic bag every 3–4 days to help ventilate the cuttings. After 6–10 weeks, let the cuttings harden off by removing the plastic bag more regularly. After another couple of weeks, pot up in individual pots.

- Pelargonium (page 86), fuchsia (see page 69), clary sage (see page 152), lavender (see page 78), marsh mallow (see page 55), elderberry (see page 92) and catmint (see page 142).

- Why not experiment? If a plant produces lots of sideshoots, the chances are that the cuttings will take root this way and it's worth giving it a go.

HARDWOOD CUTTINGS

This is the propagation method for plants that have harder stems, such as climbers, shrubs and trees. It is a similar method to taking softwood cuttings and is best done from mid-autumn to late winter. Hardwood cuttings are easier to look after than softwood cuttings because they don't need much in the way of TLC.

Take a cutting from this year's growth, dividing the long stem into several 20–25cm (8–10in) sections and making sure you've removed the soft growing tip. Cut at an angle above the bud at the top of the cutting and make a straight cut below a pair of buds at the base of each section. Insert the cuttings into a 7cm (3in) pot filled with gritty compost and push down gently so that two-thirds of the cutting is below the surface. You should be able to fit about 5 cuttings around the edge of a pot. Leave the pot in a sheltered spot until the following autumn, checking occasionally to make sure the soil doesn't dry out.

TRY IT WITH

- Currants (see page 195), fig (see page 183) and honeysuckle (page 83).

SEMI-RIPE CUTTINGS

This technique, which is best done at the end of the summer, can be used for lots of herbs, as well as shrubs, trees and climbers. A combination of the two other types of cuttings, you're taking a cutting from this year's growth, which is hard at the bottom and soft at the top. Take cuttings in the same way that you would for softwood cuttings but make them a bit bigger, around 10–15cm (4–6in).

Insert the cutting in a 7cm (3in) pot filled with a mixture of half compost and half perlite or sharp sand. You should be able to fit about 5 cuttings around the edge of a pot. Cover the pot with a plastic bag. While the cuttings won't need bottom heat if they were taken while the weather is still warm, they'll benefit from the comfort of a glasshouse or windowsill out of direct sunlight.

TRY IT WITH

- Bay (see page 133), anise hyssop (see page 52), lavender (see page 78), rosemary (see page 150), sage (see page 155), thyme (see page 159), tea camellia (see page 117).

GROWING UNDER GLASS

There are some brilliant books dedicated to growing under glass and I don't presume to share all the information they would cover in this section. However, there are some rules that will make a difference if you're lucky enough to have a glasshouse or conservatory, and these rules also apply if you're growing plants on a windowsill.

GROWING PLANTS IN A GLASSHOUSE

There are a few things to consider if you've inherited a glasshouse with your home or are planning to buy one for your plot. If you're buying a new glasshouse, think about the site; it needs to be as sunny as possible and preferably not in the shadow of a building or a tree (in addition to shade, the tree will also cause problems if it sheds its leaves). Ideally your glasshouse should stand on foundations, even if they're just paving stones, so your site needs to allow for this. As a general rule of thumb, choose the biggest glasshouse that will fit in your garden that you can afford because once you get the taste for growing under glass you'll never look back.

The principal difference between growing outdoors and under glass is that you can largely control the climate in a glasshouse. Certainly, you can provide warmer and more humid conditions in a glasshouse to suit plants that wouldn't survive in the great outdoors and also help seedlings get off to an earlier start than if they were sown outside.

While we tend to think of soaring temperatures inside a glasshouse, part of the requirement is maintaining a stable temperature for plants, which won't thank you if they're cold in spring and autumn and boiling hot in the summer. You will need to monitor the temperature with a minimum/ maximum thermometer and vary the temperature as required, providing additional heat if necessary or altering ventilation and shade to cool things down. Ventilating your glasshouse can be as simple as opening the doors, windows and vents or as sophisticated as having an automatic vent-opener that responds to changing temperatures, opening and closing as required.

Thankfully, the cost of heating a glasshouse can be tailored to suit your budget, from mains electric heaters to gas and oil burners that require a supply of fuel. Eco-friendly gardeners will prefer to use alternative methods, such as large rocks and other heat-absorbent materials that are warmed by the sun during the day and then release the heat throughout the night.

It's really important to get your watering right in a glasshouse; too much watering will cause problems with disease, while too little will harm your plants or even kill them. See page 17 for watering advice.

Keep your glasshouse as clean as possible. Piles of soil, dust and cobwebs will attract unwanted pests and harbour diseases that could harm your plants. Once you've washed the walls, floor and glass, turn your attention to your pots and equipment. A good spring-clean will make all the difference.

If you discover unwanted pests, you can make (or buy) hanging fly papers or biological controls to trap or kill them. Hanging nets over doors, vents and windows will also cut down on pests getting in. I've visited numerous glasshouses where the gardeners ingeniously grow carnivorous plants to help control glasshouse pests. To avoid problems with spider mites, which love dry heat, pour water on the glasshouse floor in the morning to provide some humidity throughout the day.

GROWING PLANTS ON A WINDOWSILL

If you're growing indoors on a windowsill, don't overcrowd your plants; give each specimen room to breathe and space for air to circulate. Don't forget to feed your plants and keep an eye on their soil to check it isn't drying out. It's worth buying a soilless compost (see page 13) to avoid issues with soil-borne diseases. Avoid using soil from the garden as it can compress down after a while, which makes watering tricky.

Choose heat-loving plants for windows that have the brightest light and most hours of sun during the short, cool winter days. Parsley (see page 149) and mint (see page 138) will cope better with east- and west-facing windows, which get their light in the morning or evenings only.

If none of your windows provide adequate light, you can rig up grow lights. As long as plants are within about a foot of the lights, it should work as well as sunlight. There is a system for setting up and acclimatizing your plants to grow lights, so follow the manufacturer's instructions for your particular brand of light.

BOTANICALS TO GROW ON A KITCHEN WINDOWSILL

Aloe vera (see page 104)

Calamondin (see page 175)

Chilli (see page 169)

Lemongrass (see page 125)

Tea camellia (see page 117)

Saffron crocus (see page 121)

Stevia (see page 156)

CONTAINERS, RAISED BEDS & BORDERS

The space you have to grow in will determine whether you choose to grow plants in containers, raised beds or borders. Ideally, you'll have a combination of all three, but for most of us that's a dream as opposed to reality.

CONTAINERS

Containers are a great solution when space is an issue. They are available in many different shapes, sizes and materials, making it easy to find something to suit your taste and budget. The web is a brilliant source for new and recycled pots and, depending on how creative you're feeling, junk shops and reclamation centres can also provide a treasure trove of possibilities. However, a word of caution: try to avoid dinky pots. As pretty and quirky as old tin cans and vintage cups and saucers are, you really have to ensure you're growing the appropriate plant for such a tiny vessel. The smaller the pot, the quicker the soil dries out and its nutrients become depleted, which means you've committed yourself to daily watering (at least) and frequent feeding to keep your plant alive. If you miss a day or two of watering and the soil dries out, you'll stress the plant and it'll start to behave oddly, either sending up long flower stems in an effort to set seed as quickly as possible before it dies or the crop will be affected due to dehydration. I realize this may sound a bit gloomy but pots that are too small are a real pet hate of mine because it can lead to frustration when plants don't survive. That said, there are some plants, like basil and thyme (see page 159), cactus and succulents, that are perfectly happy to be tucked snugly into a cup or old oil can. So, to avoid disappointment, be realistic about the amount of care and attention you can provide your containers.

It is important to consider the pros and cons of different types of container. I love pots made from concrete, terracotta and cement, though they do require extra watering and maintenance because they are porous. Containers made from these materials retain heat, which is fine for sun-seeking plants – herbs won't mind at all – but will damage other more sensitive specimens. Such containers are, of course, heavy to move, can crack in freezing conditions and often have inadequate drainage (with just one hole in the base). Fake concrete, fake terracotta and wood-effect pots made from plastic allow you to enjoy the best of both worlds – designer style and an attractive finish that's hard-wearing and, of course, light. In a small garden, it can be useful to be able to move a pot around to catch more sun, find shady shelter or a bit of winter protection. If such containers don't have drainage holes, it's easy to drill holes in the base. However, being a petroleum-based product, these plastic containers aren't an environmentally-friendly option. Metal planters are a good, lightweight option, though they will heat up in the sun and dry out the soil. If they don't have drainage holes, you'll need to drill some prior to planting.

Wood is a great material in terms of aesthetics and offers some insulation from the heat, too. However, wooden containers need maintenance in terms of staining or preserving using an eco-friendly product every season or two. If you're considering using an old container like a barrel, check that it isn't covered in a chemical preservative that's unsuitable for growing edibles. It's important to make sure wooden containers are made from a sustainable wood source.

RAISED BEDS

Raised beds are the next best thing to having borders in your garden because they provide a large space for plants. The beds don't need to be built on top of soil; if you have a paved courtyard, you can simply place a raised bed frame on the ground and fill it with soil. Raised beds are a good solution if you have poor or heavy soil that is hard to transform into a workable loam-based medium.

BOTANICALS FOR CONTAINERS & BASKETS

Alpine strawberry (see page 184)

Anise hyssop (see page 52)

Blueberries: blueberry, bilberry, huckleberry & honeyberry (see page 200)

Cardamom (see page 126)

Chilean guava (see page 199)

Comfrey (see page 96)

Cucumber (see page 179)

Currants (see page 195)

Hibiscus (see page 73)

Juniper (see page 76)

Liquorice (see page 130)

Rosemary (see page 150)

Sweetfern (see page 62)

Turmeric (see page 122)

Viola (see page 100)

Wasabi (see page 202)

Wormwood (see page 56)

PLANTING COMBINATIONS

When selecting plants, the most important principle is to find the right plant for the right place. Choose plants that are hardy and can cope if you ignore them for a bit and leave them to go thirsty. Check your plants as often as you can – every day is ideal, though it's not always practical – and take care of them so they can reward you with harvestable crops and colourful displays for as long as possible. Make the most of your vertical space by choosing hanging or climbing habits or experiment with plants that might appear to need space but can cope just as well being trained up-and-over something. If you don't have a lot of room to play with, often the best idea is to grow crops and plants in containers. You can even grow trees and shrubs in containers, just so long as you can give them the biggest pot your space and budget allows. Containers can also make life easier for you if you've got plants that need different types of soils or different aspects, and they're surprisingly versatile, too. For my previous book, I grew selections of fruit and vegetables that could be harvested to create a one-pot dish. If making face cream excites you, why not grow the ingredients for a couple of different types of face cream together? Or, if you love herbal teas, consider creating a pot that provides a selection of flavourful leaves and flowers. Grouping plants like this can make the most of space and create a talking point and pretty display at the same time. However, always make sure the plants you choose to grow together have the same needs, including the amount of sunshine they can tolerate, soil type and whether they overwinter or not.

Bricks or pressure-treated or tanalized timber are the best materials to use if you're building your own raised beds, though you can also buy ready-to-go raised bed packs. It's worth marking out the area for your bed before you start building to ensure the corners are square and the ground is level. If you're using wood, insert retaining stakes in the corners so you can attach the side lengths to them. Aim to have sides that are about 20cm (8in) high. Put a layer of stones, broken bricks, etc. at the bottom of the bed for drainage if the bed is on paving or hard, clay soil, followed by the best-quality soil your budget allows. Dig in plenty of well-rotted organic matter and let it all settle for a couple of weeks before planting.

BORDERS

Borders are ideal for planting, as long as the soil isn't too poor. To prepare the bed, dig over the soil and remove any weeds and old roots. Add plenty of well-rotted organic matter and, if the soil is heavy clay, horticultural grit to help open up the structure.

Think about edging the border to help keep the soil from spilling out onto the lawn or paving. You can use bricks, stones, tiles or special plastic edging, as well as a natural edge created by low-growing compact plants. Depending on the size of your border, you can shape your edges, too. Use curves to create a sense of space and neat, straight lines if you prefer the impression of order, though they can make your garden appear smaller.

GATHERING WITH FRIENDS – SCENTED BOTANICALS

If you're able to squeeze a table and some chairs into your garden, don't miss the opportunity to surround them with deliciously scented plants. Wafts of sweet-smelling flowers can really add to the atmosphere and transport you to balmy summer's evenings you've enjoyed on holiday. If you enjoy cooking and eating outside, growing your favourite herbs and adding fresh snippets of them to food or drinks can add a new dimension to alfresco dining. String up a few lights, fire up the barbecue, make some cocktails and you're away…

Scented plants can turn your garden into a haven, and, of course, they can be used in the kitchen or for homemade remedies, thus completely earning their space in your garden. In addition to herbs like lemon verbena, lavender and chamomile, which emit a heady fragrance when their leaves are rubbed gently, there are other scented plants to add to the mix that will come into their own when the sun sets. Moths and other insects of the night love such plants. Jasmine, honeysuckle and *Dianthus* 'Mrs Sinkins' will all twinkle in the gloaming. Position them within arm's reach, where you can stroke them to release their heady scent, and you'll find yourself wanting to eat every meal outdoors.

SCENTED BOTANICALS

Bergamot (see page 84)

English lavender (see page 78)

Honeysuckle (see page 83)

Garden pinks & carnations (see page 64)

Indian mint (see page 139)

Lemon verbena (see page 106)

Roman chamomile (see page 60)

Sage (see page 155)

GROWING ON A BALCONY

(OR YOUR DOORSTEP OR ANY OTHER SMALL SPOT)

The first flat I rented as an adult was a top-floor affair. Luckily, my flatmate wanted the larger bedroom and so was perfectly happy to let me have the box room, which had a Velux window that I could climb through to reach a 2m² (21½sq ft) flat roof. The flat roof became the site of my first attempt to create a garden. One battered wine box filled with basil and oregano was quickly joined by a variety of other herbs and colourful annuals in tins, pots and more wine boxes. These containers were balanced on the ledge outside the window and around the edges of the roof, and I even remember arranging some on top of upturned boxes to create a bit of height and give my friends and I enough room to stand, literally cheek-by-jowl, enjoying a beer in the splendour of my "rooftop" garden. I learned that you need to be diligent and patient, especially with containers, because a lot of your time is spent watering. You simply can't let them dry out or they'll perish in the first rays of summer sun. It was also useful to see that the more I picked the herbs and deadheaded the flowers, the better, more vigorous and healthier the plants became – simple, basic gardening know-how.

These days, I still like to find nooks and crannies in to which to tuck plants. If you don't have a garden or a balcony, I urge you to find other spaces for a pot or two, such as a porch, doorstep or even on top of walls.

BOTANICALS TO GROW ON A BALCONY

Burnet (see page 94)

Caraway (see page 118)

Electric daisy (see page 51)

Marigold (see page 59)

Oregano (see page 145)

Samphire (see page 176)

Stevia (see page 156)

SHADE DWELLERS

One of the tricky challenges to overcome in a small garden is that your plot probably doesn't get a lot of sun. Surprisingly, there are lots of tough specimens that will put up with the gloom and still go as far as to reward you with an edible or useable crop. They're the unsung plant heroes of the garden, if you will. It might seem odd that productive plants don't need sun. Thankfully, Mother Nature is pretty resourceful: just as there are plants that have evolved to cope with either little or no water or boggy, waterlogged soils, there are a group of optimists who won't sulk in the shade.

To make the most of your growing potential, containers are a good idea for shady spaces. If you're keen to grow something that might be happier in partial shade but the only spot you have is more dark than light, consider planting it in a container and then moving it to that far corner of the garden that gets a little sun for a few hours every now and then to pep it up.

I need to come clean with you at this point: gardening in a shady plot is not all plain sailing. Unfortunately, slugs and snails are happy to lurk in the shade so vigilance is necessary. If you're growing plants in the ground, organic pet- and child-friendly slug pellets are a must; and if you've got some containers, pot feet will help a little, as will a copper band around the base of the plant or crop in the pot. However, when it comes to dealing with slugs, you can't beat a late-night jaunt around the garden with a torch to pick off the pests, though your neighbours may think you're mad. If you're like me, disposing of the slugs and snails could be a dilemma, they are living creatures after all, but there's nothing like looking at a decimated crop first thing in the morning to harden your heart and make you swear to get your revenge. I used to throw my slugs and snails into next door's garden, which, before you judge me, was gorgeously overgrown because the house was derelict. The last laugh was on me though, as I've since discovered my actions were pretty futile because snails have a homing instinct. Further research suggest I should have lobbed them more than 20m (22 yards) away to confuse them and ensure they stayed lost. However, for most of us (and for me too, now that a lovely couple have bought the house next door and renovated the garden), chucking the pests over a fence isn't an option. These days I gather them in a pot, dash to the front of the house and tip them out onto the road to let the cars, birds, frogs and foxes do their worst. I'm not proud, I admit, but I do have very happy, healthy crops.

SHADE-LOVING BOTANICALS

Chervil (see page 111)

Carolina allspice (see page 114)

French tarragon (see page 113)

Lemon balm (see page 137)

Lovage (see page 134)

Mint (see page 138)

Parsley (see page 149)

Raspberry (see page 196)

Rhubarb (see page 192)

Thyme (see page 159)

THE TETRIS BORDER

I didn't intentionally set out to create a gimmicky border but it's often the case that a good idea comes about when you're trying to fulfil a need.

My backyard is 4.5 x 3m (15 x 10ft) – the small side of a "decent-sized" garden. One of the key issues when you're gardening in a tiny space is that you don't have room to grow lots of different plants, which can be frustrating if you've got a large number of plants you'd like to try. If you're anything like me, the temptation to plant single specimens will be strong. Indeed, for this book it was a necessity for me to plant over 80 botanicals in my garden – a tall order!

To the left of my garden, as I stand looking out at it from my kitchen, I have fitted in three raised beds, as well as a bonsai-sized (but brilliant) glasshouse and some containers filled with currants. Two of the raised beds are 1m² (10¾sq ft) and the third is 1 x 2m (3¼ x 6½ft). My garden faces east, so one of the raised beds gets a couple of hours of summer sun and is otherwise in shade, while the other two are largely in full sun. There's plenty of scope for the type of plants I can grow here; not so much when it comes to space.

While planning the larger of the three raised beds, I chopped and changed my mind, prioritizing fennel over echinacea and then reversing my decision, and so on. Eventually, it occurred to me that I could broaden out the planting of these three beds to work as a single unit in order to achieve the flow and rhythm you would strive to create in a traditional border. By splitting my three fennel plants across two beds, I created space for something else and kept the design looking cohesive by dotting them in the three separate spaces. I'm really pleased with the results.

It's a design principle that's worth considering for containers, too. Individually, each container has its own identity, but when the same plant features in several containers it helps create a cohesion that can transform your garden from a confused mash of many plants to a well-thought-out design. The resulting planting will present a sense of space and calm – a must for an after-hours haven or quiet refuge from the hustle and bustle of the city.

I played with height in the raised beds, too. I was reluctant to dedicate the border closest to the kitchen for low-growing plants, increasing the height of the plants in the next bed and keeping my statuesque beauties for the end bed. Treating the three beds as a single border helped me to be bolder with my plant choices, and once I was happy, I could tweak each one to work as a stand-alone bed, too.

IN SUMMER

It's early in the morning, the day before my son and I set off on holiday for a week. I'm excited to get away but worried about the garden. It's been a long, hot summer already and it takes a while to water my garden in the morning and evening to ensure everything is happy and looking its best for photography for this book. Thankfully, I've got an amazing friend who's popping around to see to the garden. Oh yes, and to check on our cat.

I love this time of day. We're in the city, so there are the usual bursts of noise every now and again, but my garden is private and strangely peaceful. I can hear the occasional clatter of cutlery, muffled voices and someone is playing great music, but there's a stillness, too; a sense of calm before the day gets going in earnest. If you don't already do so, I urge you to get up early and enjoy being in your garden or simply look out at it from your balcony or window. Soak it all in. It will make all your hard work feel worthwhile, and can often provide you with inspiration to finesse your plot, too.

I'm lucky today, it's already hot, which is just heavenly. Bees are buzzing – I wonder whether it's in an effort to get their work done before the heat of the day cranks up. This is a good chance to assess the raised borders. Planted in late spring, everything has had the chance to get established and now I can review what is and isn't working.

a single main stem, about 1.25m (4ft) high. Though considerably taller than the rest of the plants in the border, it doesn't overpower. It's an incredibly graceful shrub with silvery leaves and diaphanous blooms. The mallow and clary sage are alive with bees. The sweet cicely has been slow to get established and has left that corner of the raised bed looking a little sparse. I know patience is required but it's tempting to fill it with something else. I think the bed could take more great burnet as it provides such a fantastic pop of strong colour.

BED NO. 2

This border is still a work in progress, though I can imagine it will look gorgeous when it's more established. The variety of echinacea I've chosen is slow to get going, but once it does it'll provide gorgeous pink flowers that, for me, will be the stars of this border. It's a similar story with the nigella at the front, which is very delicate and almost overpowered by the bergamot. I think the nigella will hold its own next year as the self-sown seedlings should get off to an earlier start. If not, I'll move them. The combination of the burly deep-purple leaves of the shiso perilla, the anise hyssop and the fennel is looking great, and it will be even better once the fennel flowers deepen to a golden yellow. Sadly, the bergamot is suffering with powdery mildew. For now, I'm picking off the diseased leaves because I don't quite have the heart to cut it back completely, though I think I'll have to do so soon as even the new growth has the telltale white bloom. The catmint has suffered in the heat – that or the cat has been at it. A happy surprise: the silvery-white foliage of wormwood lifts the strong colours in this border and picks up the silver-green leaves of the marsh mallow. I'll find a permanent spot for wormwood in this border next year. Cabbage white butterflies, bees, hoverflies and all manner of other winged insects are dancing all over this border – they love the anise hyssop in particular.

BED NO. 1

The sweet woodruff provides a low carpet of glossy green rosettes that covers about one-third of the raised bed. It looks great against the dark grey wooden border. Droplets of early morning dew perch on the whorls of leaves, wobbling manically but not bursting as Teddy (my dog) snuffles and shovels through the leaves – I think he loves their sweet hay scent. I'd like to use sweet woodruff in the other borders as well but they get too much sun. It's creeping around the clary sage and sets off the stems of bright blooms, which are a delicate soft purple at the base and develop into vibrant blooms as they gradually open towards the top. The clary sage's brash colour and languid habit works nicely with its neighbour, *Fuchsia* 'Hawkshead'. By contrast, its foliage creates a dense, almost solid, shape that is softened by the delicate white flowers that daintily dangle all over it. The sweet woodruff has enveloped the base of the marsh mallow. At the moment the mallow is

BED NO. 3

I can't wait until next year when the angelica will be established in all its glory. It's put on good growth and has provided a few stems for me to try candying. For now the fennel towers above the other plants. It'll look even more impressive when the architectural angelica leaves help show off its effervescent umbellifers. I think I might add another hollyhock or two to introduce spots of white – though there isn't much room, their towering single spires should be easy to squeeze in. The shiso perilla loves it in this border but I'm going to take one of the two out next year to give the bergamot (*Monarda* 'Schneewittchen') more space to flourish. The clary sage is a pink form and has faded more quickly than the other ones I planted. I suspect the problem may be a bit of pet action here as it's growing next to the catmint. Given the lacklustre performance of the clary sage, I'm happy I let a rogue nasturtium seedling (*Tropaeolum majus* 'Empress of India') from last year do its thing. The pop of flaming orange really works. I've seen this countless times in show gardens, where a flash of an "accent" colour is used to great effect. It lifts and draws the eye and helps the purples and whites sing out. I might not let the nasturtium roam free next year, as I think it'll be too crowded, but I'll grow it in pots and place a few around the edge – it'll look fantastic against the angelica. Like the sweet cicely in the first border, the nasturtium was too slow to get going.

BOTANICALS FOR THE TETRIS BORDER

Angelica (see page 109)	Fennel (see page 128)	Nigella (see page 143)
Anise hyssop (see page 52)	Fuchsia (see page 69)	Sage (see page 155)
Bergamot (see page 84)	Great burnet (page 94)	Shisho perilla (see page 146)
Catmint (see page 142)	Marsh mallow (see page 55)	Sweet cicely (see page 140)
Echinacea (see page 66)	Nasturtium (see page 99)	Sweet woodruff (see page 70)

TISANES

I know it might sound a bit affected but I can't resist using the French word tisane to describe herbal tea. To my mind, if you've gone to the trouble of growing your own herbs to make a cup of tea, you've earned the right to refer to it in this rather more alluring way. It sets the tone for the whole experience: you're not just "grabbing a cuppa", you're taking the time to sit down and sip a tisane, savouring the flavour, even if it's just for five minutes. Think of it as a mini mindfulness exercise. While drinking your tea, take a few minutes to consider the effort that went into growing and harvesting the herb and preparing the drink. Simple pleasures like this deserve to be appreciated.

Tisanes are a fantastic way to boost the immune system and detoxify our bodies. Herbs are said to contain more antioxidants than fruit and vegetables, so it makes sense to start growing them. Depending on the herb, you can use some or all of the plant, including the roots, bark, stems, leaves, flowers and seeds. Each plant or part of the plant has a unique flavour or medicinal quality. Herbs can be used fresh or dried and stored for the winter, when you'll be thankful to get a herby health boost.

TISANE HOUSEKEEPING

Here are some useful tea-making guidelines. I'm drawn to the idea that there are some concrete rules when it comes to making this sort of brew.

- Don't use iron or aluminium utensils to prepare your drink as these metals meddle with the herbs' potency. Stick to stainless steel, enamelware or heatproof glass.

- Use good water. Filtering tap water to remove the smell and taste of chlorine is a good idea.

- One teaspoon of dried herbs or two teaspoons of crushed fresh herbs is the ideal quantity for a single cup of tea.

- A couple of minutes is long enough to infuse the herb in either a cup or a teapot of boiling water, before straining and serving.

- Just like a regular cuppa, using a little dried stevia or honey to sweeten the tea can improve or enhance the flavour.

- Two or three cups of tea a day is about the right amount to drink because many are diuretic to some degree.

WHICH HERBS MAKE A GOOD CUPPA?

Anise hyssop (see page 52)

Bergamot (see page 84)

Carnations (see page 64)

Catmint (see page 142)

Citrus blossoms (see page 171)

Echinacea (see page 66)

Elderflowers (see page 92)

Fennel seed (see page 128)

Hibiscus (see page 73)

Lavender (see page 78)

Lemon balm (see page 137)

Lemon verbena (see page 106)

Lemongrass (see page 125)

Marsh mallow (see page 55)

Mint (see page 138)

Nasturtium (see page 99)

Raspberry leaves (see page 196)

Roman chamomile (see page 60)

Rosemary (see page 150)

Sage (see page 155)

Sweet woodruff (see page 70)

Thyme (see page 159)

MY FAVOURITE TISANES FOR THE MOST COMMON COMPLAINTS

INSOMNIA
(DON'T GET ME STARTED ON THIS SUBJECT!)

Catmint (see page 142)

Lavender (see page 78)

Lemon balm (see page 137)

Roman chamomile (see page 60)

Spearmint (see page 138)

DETOX

Citrus (see page 171)

Fennel (see page 128)

Parsley (see page 149)

Peppermint (see page 138)

Rosehip (see page 88)

Turmeric (see page 122)

DIGESTION

Fennel (see page 128)

Lemongrass (see page 125)

Liquorice root (see page 130)

Peppermint (see page 138)

Turmeric (see page 122)

ANTI-EEYORE
(OR HAPPINESS HERBS)

Lemon balm (see page 137)

Lemon verbena (see page 106)

Roman chamomile (see page 60)

Rosemary (see page 150)

Thyme (see page 159)

CLASSIC COMBOS

There's a charming idea that for a well-balanced drink you need to combine something that's green with something full-bodied in flavour. Try parsley (see page 149), sage (see page 155) and catmint (see page 142) for the 'green' element. If you want big-hitting fragrance, use herbs like rosemary (see page 150), thyme (see page 159), lemon verbena (see page 106) and mint (see page 138). Flowers will add colour, as well as introducing a floral note. Rose petals (see page 88) are an obvious choice, along with chamomile (see page 60) and violas (see page 100). Play around with these three groups to find the flavour that most suits your mood and taste.

HERBAL INFUSIONS: WHEN IS A TEA NOT A TEA?

Herbal infusions are generally stronger than a refreshing cup of herbal tea. A good ratio is 25g (1oz) dried herb (flower and/or leaves) to 568ml (1 pint) water. To make an infusion, bring the water to the boil, add the herb and immediately remove from the heat, cover with a lid and let steep for 15 minutes. Strain and serve.

HOW TO DRY LEAVES

As with most things homemade, the flavour of homegrown dried herbs will be far superior to shop-bought versions, so don't let your herbs go to waste; have a go at drying them. There are several methods, but essentially the process is easy as herbs don't contain too much moisture. Stored properly, dried herbs won't be contaminated by bacteria, mould or yeast and can be used for up to 12 months.

Pick leaves, flowers or ripe seed heads early in the morning before the sun has evaporated any of the essential oils. I'm assuming you won't have used any chemicals, so they won't need to be washed.

Air-drying is exactly as it sounds, though humidity isn't your friend when it comes to dehydrating herbs. If you live somewhere humid, this isn't the method for you. If you are drying large quantities of herbs, hang them upside down in bunches somewhere warm and dry. In fact, hanging the herbs outdoors during the summer is best, but only if you can guarantee the weather will stay hot and dry over a period of a few weeks. Otherwise, find somewhere warm and dry indoors to hang your herbs. Wrap a paper or muslin bag loosely around bunches of herbs. I tend to use string to tie the stems but recently I've read that a tie-twist allows you to tighten the bunches as they shrink, which sounds like a sensible idea.

Making or buying a drying frame, by which I mean a wooden frame with muslin stretched between the wood, is a better option for drying herbs, but it does take up more room. Lay the herbs individually across the muslin and turn every 12 hours or so.

Ovens can be used to dry herbs, but only if the oven can be set as low as 38ºC (100ºF). To test your herbs are dry, crumble them between your fingertips.

Store dried herbs in sterilized airtight jars out of direct sunshine.

HOMEMADE BOOZE

Over the years, I've made my fair share of sloe gin (see page 191) and damson vodka. I love the process: picking the fruits at the end of summer, returning to the kitchen to wash them and then steeping them in alcohol, religiously turning the bottles throughout the autumn, and looking forward to the festive parties when the bottles will be opened and enjoyed with friends.

While these familiar wintry tipples are delicious, I wanted to expand my booze repertoire for this book. This turned out to be an easy task, thanks to a cool independent microdistillery that's just a 15-minute walk from my house. Danny Walker, co-owner of Psychopomp Microdistillery, is something of a spirit evangelist. While he and his team make a pretty fantastic craft gin, Danny is totally brilliant at spreading the word about making and flavouring it. A few minutes after meeting him, two things become evidently clear: first, he truly LOVES what he does (then again, who wouldn't?), and secondly, there isn't much he doesn't know about Mother's Ruin or, it turns out, a whole range of other spirits.

The good news, for those of us who grow botanicals but might not have a copper still tucked away on a kitchen shelf, is that it's possible to produce very drinkable liqueurs using very simple methods – essentially, flavouring the spirit with botanicals or creating tinctures (macerating an individual botanical in a high-alcohol spirit – vodka, to you and me) and combining these in your chosen spirit.

DIY GIN

Danny was keen to get across that there really aren't any rules when it comes to crafting your own booze. Sure, gin, for example, has to be flavoured with juniper – its name is derived from *jeneverbes*, the Dutch word for "juniper berry", but that's about it. For purists, perfectionists and traditionalists (depending on how you look at it), there are three other base flavours that comprise the classic gin recipe: coriander seeds, to provide citrus notes; angelica root, to add a woody, earthy layer; and liquorice root, as a natural sweetener. (These are the "Fab Four" ingredients in Gordon's and Tanqueray gin). However, after that it's about having fun and working out what you do and don't like. It's about experimenting and – wait for it – tasting as you go along. So grab yourself a bottle of vodka, a handful of your favourite botanicals and see how it goes.

A good tip is to start by experimenting with small amounts of gin and keeping a note of the ratio of botanicals to the spirit, so you can scale-up production once you hit on a great recipe. The longer you leave the botanicals to steep, the stronger they will taste. As a rule of thumb, potent flavourings might only need a few days, whereas mild or subtle herbs might benefit from a few weeks – remember, taste and test the flavours as you go. Once your flavoured gin is ready, strain the liquid and then pass it through a muslin cloth and transfer to sterilized bottles.

THE BOTANICAL GARDEN

DIY VERMOUTH

It turns out that we botanical growers are primed to make vermouth, too. Just like juniper is an essential ingredient for gin, you need wormwood to make vermouth. In fact, it's illegal to call a spirit vermouth if it doesn't include wormwood. Other than that, the sky's the limit when it comes to flavouring this spirit. One maker of craft vermouth boasts 20 botanicals.

Before you can start to flavour vermouth, you need to prepare a collection of tinctures (see opposite). Once they're ready, you're ready for the off. Pour a bottle of white wine into a saucepan, add 200g (7oz) caster sugar and heat until the sugar dissolves. (Alternatively, replace the caster sugar with homemade caramel for a deeper, darker flavour.) Remove from the heat and let it cool. Once the liquid has cooled down, begin adding your chosen tinctures – use a pipette and go slowly, adding one drop of individual flavour at a time, tasting and recording quantities as you go.

DIY BITTERS

I was excited to discover I could make my own bitters. It requires a combination of bitter and aromatic herbs as well as some exotic spices (most of which are difficult or near-impossible to grow in the UK), so you may need to play a bit fast and loose with a combination of homegrown herbs and shop-bought spices if you really get into making bitters. However, simple recipes can be created using ingredients you can harvest from your own backyard.

Bittering agents include angelica, liquorice root and wormwood. You can complement these bitters with aromatics and spices like caraway, cardamom, chamomile, chilli, citrus peel, coriander seeds, fennel, juniper berries, hibiscus, lavender, lemongrass, mint, rose, rosemary, sage and thyme. As a general rule, you're aiming to create a blend with about 20–50 per cent bitters with herbs and spices to round out the flavour.

To create your own recipe, combine individual tinctures of herbs and spices (see opposite). To taste your concoction, add a few drops of your bitters to still or sparkling water. The concentrate should be very bitter.

ORIGINS OF SPIRITS

It may surprise you to discover that aperitifs like gin, vermouth and absinthe were originally intended as medicinal drinks. Botanicals chosen to soothe upset stomachs and chest infections (gin) or to help digestion (vermouth and absinthe) were steeped in wine and drunk by men, women and children alike. Over time, the recipes were tweaked, the base alcohol evolved and the world's penchant for spirits firmly took hold... but that's a story for a different book.

TIPPLE TIP

You can flavour any base spirit, though white ones are often best, so try rum, vodka and gin. Brandy and whiskeys are more complex and it's harder to create a balanced, palatable drink, though it's still very much worth having a go.

TINCTURES

A tincture is a concentrated herbal extract that is made by infusing fresh or dried flowers, leaves, roots, bark or berries in a high-proof alcohol (otherwise known as vodka). Steeping herbs in alcohol before consuming them can help our bodies obtain the beneficial compounds found in herbs, many of which our digestive system can't extract when we simply eat the fresh herbs. Heat also does the trick most of the time (think herbal teas) but using a tincture is a good alternative to have up our sleeve.

Tinctures are left to infuse for much longer than you would steep a herbal tea, which means that you don't need to consume very much to get the same benefit – a drop or two as opposed to a cup (or more) of tea.

To make a tincture, gather together a collection of sterilized airtight jars – you'll need as many jars as you have varieties of herbs. The quantity of herbs you use to make a tincture will vary depending on which part of the plant you're using and whether they're fresh or dried.

- For fresh leaves and flowers: fill two-thirds of a jar with chopped or ground fresh leaves or flowers.

- For dried herbs: fill half a jar with finely chopped dried herbs.

- For dried roots, barks and berries: fill one-third of a jar with finely chopped dried roots, barks or berries.

Fill the rest of the jar with vodka. Label the jars and let infuse in a cool dark place for 6–8 weeks, shaking the jars daily. When you're happy with the flavour, strain through muslin, squeezing out every last drop of liquid to ensure you've got all the herb compound. Transfer to amber bottles and store in the refrigerator. The tinctures should keep for up to one year. You can use the tinctures neat, diluted in tea or soft drinks, or you can use them to flavour alcohol and cocktails.

MAKING BEAUTY PRODUCTS

As a teenager, I loved soaking in the bath and, much to the amusement of my family, I'd add slices of lemon and orange to the bathwater. Apart from essentially luxuriating in an alcohol-free cocktail, I'm not quite sure what I hoped to achieve by bathing with citrus fruit. However, it turns out I had the right idea. These days I grow many different herbs, flowers, shrubs and trees and I've discovered I can use them to make some lovely remedies that can do all manner of things, including soothe muscles, relieve headaches and even make my hair lovely and shiny.

One of the most important benefits of making homemade remedies with homegrown plants is that the final products are free from all the horrible additives and chemicals you find in non-organic, shop-bought products. In this section, I've provided you with some basic guidance for creating your own beauty products. Generally, I've stuck to recipes that are easy to make because, if you're like me, you won't have lots of spare time and won't want to buy oodles of kit just to produce a lip balm, for example. I hope you'll take these suggestions as a starting point from which you can experiment with making beauty products with floral and foliage ingredients from your own garden.

There are some incredible books available on the subject of homemade remedies (see the Bibliography, page 208) and the internet is a wonderful source of information, too, with videos and step-by-step guides. So if you find yourself getting hooked on the suggestions in this section, I strongly advise you to have a browse and try other ideas for homemade beauty products. Remember, homemade beauty products have a shorter shelf life as they don't contain preservatives, so make sure you store them in a cool, dark place.

DIY TONERS

Homemade floral toners are gentle cleansers for the skin that will clean and shrink pores and can also help redress natural pH levels for certain skin types. Toner should be applied to the skin – using cotton wool or by spritzing directly onto skin – after you've washed your face and before moisturising.

Cucumber and green tea toner: Combines equal quantities of cucumber juice (I used the juice of 3 'Crystal Lemon' cucumbers, see page 179) and green tea (which you can make from the leaves of the tea camellia, see page 117) with 1 tablespoon of vodka. Store in the fridge for up to 3 days.

Floral water toner: I couldn't resist this recipe because it looks so pretty and somehow encapsulates the idea behind the book. To make this gentle skin freshener that's good for oily skin, put 5 tablespoons rose petals, 4 tablespoons sage leaves, 3 tablespoons raspberry leaves and 2 tablespoons rosemary leaves into a jar without a metal lid and add 200ml (7fl oz) hot apple cider vinegar. Seal the jar and let steep for 2 weeks, shaking daily. Strain into a bowl and add 150ml (5fl oz) rosewater (see below), then transfer to a separate jar without a metal lid. Store in a dark, cool place or the fridge for up to 7 days.

DIY FLOWER WATERS

SIMPLE ROSEWATER

The simplest way to make rosewater is to put the petals from 3 or 4 homegrown roses (or roses from a reputable and organic source) in a small saucepan, add 300ml (10fl oz) distilled water and bring to the boil, then immediately reduce the heat

which is known as a herbal hydrosol, has toning and healing qualities, and it can be used in beauty products or added to your cooking. As a rule of thumb, about 25g (1oz) plant material will yield about 125ml (4fl oz) flower water.

Place a heatproof glass bowl in a heavy-bottomed saucepan, arrange rose petals (or other types of petal or, indeed, chopped herbs) in the saucepan around the outside of the bowl and cover the petals with distilled water. Place the saucepan's lid upside down on top of the bowl. Bring the distilled water to the boil, then add ice cubes on top of the upturned lid and reduce the heat to a simmer. (As the water simmers, flower water will collect in the glass bowl). Simmer for about 30 minutes, keeping an eye on the level of the distilled water in the saucepan and topping up if necessary so that the petals don't burn, adding extra ice cubes to the upturned lid as the original ones melt. Decant the flower water into sterilized glass jars and store in the refrigerator, where it will keep for a couple of weeks.

and simmer for 30 minutes or until the petals have lost their colour. Strain the mixture and store the rosewater in a sealed jar. Store in a cool place or the fridge for up to 7 days. if the water becomes cloudy or the aroma changes, throw it away and make a fresh batch.

DIY INFUSED OILS

While it's possible to make concentrated essential oils at home (the type commonly used in aromatherapy), the process is fairly involved and requires specialist equipment as the oils are extracted by chemicals or hot steam. Infused oils are much easier to make and can be used to create a range of beauty products. Although infused oils are less potent than essential oils, they still contain the beneficial properties needed for some remedies. The easiest way to make infused oils is to put dried

ROSE HYDROSOL

Another way to make rosewater (and other flower waters) is to create a DIY still. The main difference between this and the simple method left is that you need a few more bits of kit, namely a heatproof glass bowl and ice cubes. The resulting flower water,

FLOWERS TO MAKE FLOWER WATER

Bergamot (see page 84)	Pelargoniums (see page 86)	Peppermint (see page 138)
Chamomile (see page 60)	Juniper (see page 76)	Rose (see page 88)
Clary sage (see page 152)	Lavender (see page 78)	Rosemary (see page 150)

herbs or chopped fresh herbs of your choice – individually or a combination of flavours – in a jar and cover with a carrier oil. Olive oil is thought to be the best as it's less likely to go rancid, but coconut, jojoba, sunflower, grape seed, apricot and almond oils are good alternatives. Roughly speaking, you need double the quantity of oil to plant material. Add a circle of wax paper to the inside of the lid to help prevent chemicals from the lid interacting with the oil, seal the jar and place it on a sunny windowsill for 1 month – the sun not only helps speed up the infusion process, it helps extract beneficial properties from the herbs, too. Strain the oil and store in a sterilized jar. The infused oil should last up to 1 year, but if it starts to smell odd, discard and make a fresh batch.

DIY HAIR RINSE

I love shiny hair and homemade rinses seem to do the trick. They're super easy to make: all you need to do is put 1 teaspoon dried herb, such as rosemary, bay, marigold or chamomile, in a bowl with 250ml (9fl oz) boiling water and 1 tablespoon apple cider vinegar (the smell of which quickly disappears once on hair) and let steep for 15 minutes. Strain and let the infusion cool. Use the infusion to rinse your hair after washing it.

DIY LIP BALM

I was fascinated to discover the basic ingredients for a lip balm are oil and beeswax. While you can get fancy by adding colours (hibiscus flowers or powdered beetroot, for example) and flavours (honey), to make a really good moisturising lip balm, put 4 tablespoons grated beeswax and 3 tablespoons of your chosen infused oil (see left) or a combination thereof in a heatproof glass bowl. Set the bowl over a saucepan of simmering water, making sure the base of the bowl doesn't touch the water, and heat until the beeswax has melted. Pour into chapstick cylinders or small tins, seal and leave to set. Store in a cool, dark place for up to 6 months.

HERBS FOR INFUSED OILS

Carnations (see page 64) are good for soothing skin.

Comfrey (see page 96) will heal rashes, minor burns and insect bites.

Echinacea (see page 66) will boost the immune system and is useful when colds and flu do the rounds.

Lavender (see page 78) is calming and antifungal.

Lemon balm (see page 137) has antibacterial properties.

Marigold (see page 59) is a great healer, especially for sunburn and rashes.

Peppermint (see page 138) will soothe headaches.

Roman chamomile (see page 60) is calming and antifungal.

Rosemary (see page 150) can be added to shampoo to help with dandruff.

Thyme (see page 159) has antibacterial and antifungal properties.

Violas (see page 100) can treat dry skin, insect bites and varicose veins.

FLOWERS & SHRUBS

The plants that feature in this chapter brings to mind the adage, the old ones are the best – you might expect to find the much-loved and incredibly useful marigold, echinacea, garden pink and rose in a botanical garden. However, I couldn't resist squeezing in a few unexpected varieties, like sea buckthorn, sweet fern and shisho perilla, which I think are on track to become modern classics! Either way, I hope you'll be inspired to try growing as many of them as you can.

ELECTRIC DAISY

(ACMELLA OLERACEA)

I tried my first buzz button (one of the common names for the edible flower buds of *Acmella oleracea*) when I was interviewing a gardener who grew the most amazing array of crops for an award-winning local restaurant. As we wandered between rows of chicory and dwarf peas, he stooped down to pick a bud for me to taste from this new plant he was trying out. The experience of eating the button-shaped bud was just like a mini electric shock combined with a strange citrus-flavoured numbing sensation that lasted several minutes. Put it this way, while I didn't ask for another, I've since read about a few fun-sounding recipes that play with the bud's characteristic "zing", and I even found a couple of home remedies. So, the electric daisy is my gift to you: you can use it as a green-fingered party trick that goes something like, "Try this edible flower dipped in chocolate."

GROW ⬤ H 0.1–0.5M; W 0.1–0.5M

The electric daisy is an annual that can be sown from seed in spring. Providing your seedlings with added warmth will help them get off to a better start, eventually producing bigger plants and more flowers. I kept my seedlings in the glasshouse until the first flowers appeared, but they would have been perfectly happy on a windowsill. The seeds can also be direct-sown outdoors in early summer. Whether you grow in a container or in the border, this plant wants a rich soil and plenty of sunshine.

CARE

Pinch out young seedlings to encourage bushy plants. Feed regularly and keep plants watered.

PESTS & DISEASES

No issues.

HARVEST & STORAGE

Pick the buds once they've reached full colour – a rich golden yellow – and they can be picked all summer long. The dried plant, especially the dried flower buds, retains its "zing" for up to a year after harvesting.

HOME REMEDIES

The electric daisy, also known as the toothache plant, contains high levels of a pain-relieving agent called spilanthol, which acts as an anaesthetic. The plant can be used to make a tincture to help relieve mouth ulcers and sore throats.

I've read that this plant is the new darling of the beauty industry, providing a natural Botox-like effect in expensive face creams.

CULINARY USES

For nearly 10 years, chefs in the US have been using this plant to heighten the taste of dishes and cocktails – they simply ask diners to eat a bud before eating or drinking. Why not do the same with your friends at the next party you throw? The flower accentuates the fruity flavour of citrus-based cocktails in particular.

ANISE HYSSOP

(AGASTACHE FOENICULUM)

Anise hyssop is a real workhorse, providing plenty of perky green foliage and spikes of lilac flowers. This rather lovely perennial is great for container-growing, and would look good planted on its own or with lavender (see page 78), burnet (see page 94) or sage (see page 155). It really looked the business grown alongside the deep-purple and bronze-green leaves of the shiso perilla (see page 146) in my Tetris border (see page 32).

While I love the aniseed-scented leaves of anise hyssop, bees and butterflies are pretty partial to its nectar-rich flowers, too, which is why the plant is also known as the wonder honey plant. It's widely used in commercial honey production, which isn't surprising when you consider that an acre of this plant can support 100 beehives.

GROW ⬥ H 0.5–1M; W 0.1–0.5M

Sow seeds in a glasshouse in autumn for the following year or sow them directly in the ground in spring. Choose a sunny spot with well-drained soil and spread some grit around the base of the plant to help prevent the crown rotting.

CARE

Anise hyssop doesn't need much in the way of water or food, unless there's been a prolonged dry spell. Feel free to leave the faded flower stems on the plant until early spring so the birds can enjoy the seeds and you can enjoy the structural shape of the dried seedheads. At the start of the growing season, remove frost-bitten stems by cutting them back to

the ground to make way for fresh growth. After a few years, lift and divide plants.

PESTS & DISEASES

Powdery mildew can be a problem. If you have a country garden, anise hyssop is unpalatable to rabbits and deer.

HARVEST & STORAGE

Pick young growth and use fresh.

HOME REMEDIES

Make an infusion of the leaves and add it to your bath to treat sunburn or fungal conditions, such as athlete's foot or yeast overgrowth. The mild-flavoured flowers, freshly picked from the plant, can be chewed to freshen breath or made into a tea to help with anxiety.

CULINARY USES

The leaves can be used to flavour cold drinks or to make a tasty tea. I love this recipe for chai from *Sunset* magazine's website that suggests you infuse ¼ cup (about 20 leaves) nutmeg-scented geranium leaves and 3 anise hyssop flowers in 250ml (9fl oz) boiling water for 15 minutes, then strain the infusion into two mugs, top up each mug with 125ml (4fl oz) hot black tea and add milk and sugar to taste, but feel free to experiment with amounts to suit your tastes.

Anise hyssop leaves can also be infused in vodka, used to make a tasty syrup for flavouring cocktails or perhaps make a more liquorice-tasting mint jelly using hyssop leaves? The seeds can be used in cookies and muffins to give an aniseed flavour.

MARSH MALLOW

(ALTHAEA OFFICINALIS)

The thought of making marshmallows using the gooey substance (mucilage) found in the root of this plant guaranteed it as one of the botanicals in this book. The fact that the marsh mallow is a seriously pretty shrub is a bonus. I love the combination of the palest-pink flowers and velvety, silvery green-grey foliage. I can imagine that all but the most grungy flower fairies demand that their skirts and hats are made from its petals and leaves.

GROW ⬢ H 1.5-2.5M; W 1-1.5M

Plant the mallow in a sheltered but sunny position in moist but well-draining soil – think marshes, as the name implies. Given its height and spread, the mallow is a good plant for the back for a border. It can also be grown in a container. If you are growing it from seed, it's a good idea to sow under cover in mid-summer, ready to plant out in spring the following season.

CARE

My mallow suffered after a particularly stormy night, so be prepared to stake your plants to prevent the flower-laden stems flopping over and smothering their next-door neighbours. Feed twice a week during the summer. Cut back after flowering and pot up self-sown seedlings. The plants can be divided in spring or autumn, placing the potted-up divisions in a lightly shaded position in a cold frame or glasshouse. Alternatively, you can take root cuttings in mid winter.

PESTS & DISEASES

Flea beetle and rust.

HARVEST & STORAGE

The root is best harvested from a 2-year old plant, either in the spring before the stems shoot up or in the autumn after the leaves have dropped. Chop pieces of the root and dry them, then grind to a powder. The powder can then be used to make beauty products, like facemasks as well as medicinal lozenges. The leaves should be harvested in late summer, when the plant is just coming into flower, and they can be dried for later use.

HOME REMEDIES

A tea made from the flowers, leaves and root is traditionally used as a gargle to relieve mouth and throat ulcers and sore throats.

CULINARY USES

The marshmallow sweets we eat today actually date back to a version eaten in Ancient Egyptian times. They used to be made by combining mucilage (a thickening agent extracted from the root of the marsh mallow) with beaten egg whites and sugar. To obtain the gelatine-like mucilage, you need to simmer the roots in water for about 30 minutes, then strain the mixture.

The water left over after you've cooked any part of the plant can be used as an egg-white substitute for making meringues or mayonnaise.

WORMWOOD

(ARTEMISIA ABSINTHIUM)

I love this perennial's feathery-textured silver leaves that form a lovely mound. Even though this plant's name is said to come from the Greek word *absinthion*, which means "undrinkable", its association with absinthe made it a must-have plant for this book. I was initially worried about the idea that absinthe could make you go a little mad because it contains thujones that can stimulate the nervous system. (I was thinking of the story about Van Gogh cutting off his ear while under the influence of absinthe.) However, after chatting to a brilliant and knowledgeable maker of craft absinthe, I felt confident this was just a myth and you'd have to drink enormous quantities for any adverse side-effects – and I'm assuming that we all drink alcohol responsibly. Great stuff. Absinthe is back on the list for Christmas gifts.

GROW ⬭ H 0.5-1M; W 0.5-1M

Wormwood might be better in an individual container as its roots secrete a growth-inhibiting toxin that can stunt or kill off susceptible neighbouring plants. If you'd like it in the border, keep it at a distance from other plants, perhaps using it as a hedge around the border's edge.

This plant prefers a sunny spot in well-drained soil that isn't too rich. If you're in a very hot, sunny climate, provide the plant with some afternoon shade. If you like its silvery-toned leaves, treating it a bit mean with more sun and less water will do the trick; plants with more shade and water tend to have greener foliage. Wormwood is happy to be moved.

It's a self-seeder, so keep the plant in check if you're tight for space and don't want it to take over.

CARE

Pruning in early to mid-spring allows time for new growth to mature and flower in the same year. Snip off flowers to encourage better leaf production.

PESTS & DISEASES

White rust, downy and powdery mildews and fungal leaf disease.

HARVEST & STORAGE

Cut young growth and use fresh.

HOME REMEDIES

Wormwood has been used for centuries to treat intestinal parasites, which is how this herb got its common name. You can drink wormwood tea (use $1/2$ or 1 teaspoon of dried leaves) to relieve the symptoms of a cold or flu, though the tea's quite bitter, so you might want to sweeten it or blend the wormwood with other herbs like peppermint (see page 138) or anise hyssop (see page 52). If you find pure wormwood tea is too bitter for you to drink, try spraying it on plants as a natural insecticide or on yourself to ward off mosquitos and other biting insects. The leaves can even be used as a deterrent for clothes moths.

CULINARY USES

Wormwood is a must-have ingredient for homemade vermouth (see page 42) and absinthe and it's a jolly useful herb for creating bitters, too (see page 42). In the past, when hops were in short supply, wormwood was added to home-brewed beer.

MARIGOLD

(CALENDULA OFFICINALIS)

As long as I've grown vegetables, I've also grown marigolds. To be clear, when I say "marigolds" I mean *Calendula officinalis* and not *Tagetes spp.*, otherwise known as French marigolds. While the latter are perfectly fine bedding plants (though, to be honest, I think they're on the gaudy side of tasteful), they aren't edible.

While you can eat, drink and bathe with marigolds, they also make brilliant companion plants, attracting pollinating insects with their bright blooms. Their roots are even said to help purify soil. 'Indian Prince' is my absolute favourite, with its dark centre and rich orange flowers, and I never tire of how it lifts contrasting colours in a border or container display.

GROW ⬙ H 0.5-1M; W 0.1-0.5M

These guys don't need much pampering; they'll do just as well in poor soil and a bit of shade as they will in full sun. Sow the seeds wherever you want them to grow, either in a pot or in the ground in spring or autumn.

CARE

Deadhead fading flowers to ensure a succession of blooms from summer right through to the first frosts.

PESTS & DISEASES

Aphids and powdery mildew.

HARVEST & STORAGE

Snip off fully open flowers as needed and use fresh or dried.

HOME REMEDIES

Dried flowers can be used in tinctures (see page 43) and to make a tea that is good for stomach upsets, cramps and ulcers and can be used as a gargle for toothache and sore throats. You can infuse the fresh flowers in olive or grapeseed oil to make beauty products such as salves and creams or bath oil (see page 46). If you don't like oily bathwater, add marigold-infused water to your bathwater instead.

CULINARY USES

Marigold petals are the poor man's saffron. You can use them to decorate cakes, garnish salads and pep up butter and cream cheese.

✿ TOP TIP

Infuse marigold leaves and flowers in water (see page 46) to make an insecticidal spray to rid your prized plants from unwanted pests.

ROMAN CHAMOMILE

(CHAMAEMELUM NOBILE)

Ever since reading Mary Wesley's novel *The Camomile Lawn*, I've promised myself that at some point I will have a chamomile lawn of my own. The idea of treading on the soft, feathery foliage and being enveloped in an apple-like fragrance sounds dreamy. On a more practical note, a chamomile lawn can be a decorative solution if you have a small patch of lawn that isn't doing well.

If a chamomile lawn is too much of leap for you, or you don't have space for a lawn, go for a large container planted with chamomile so you can enjoy a green fix, pretty flowers, a heavenly scent and a useful crop. Butterflies

and bees will appreciate chamomile too. If shade is an issue, you could try growing creeping thyme (*Thymus serpyllum*) instead.

I chose two varieties of chamomile for my garden: *Chamaemelum nobile* 'Treneague', also known as lawn chamomile, which is a carpet-forming variety that doesn't produce flowers, and *C. nobile*, which is also carpet-forming but grows a little taller and produces pretty flowers. If you're just looking to make chamomile tea, Jekka McVicar suggests wild or German chamomile (*Matricaria recutita*), which has an apple-flavour and doesn't need to be sweetened with honey.

GROW ⬳ H 0.1–0.5M; W 0.1–0.5M

Roman chamomile needs bright light conditions. A little dappled shade is okay, but the plant won't appreciate lurking in the dark for hours on end. If your front window gets the sun, grow chamomile in a window box.

If you're planting directly into the ground, make sure the soil is neither too sandy nor too heavy and clay-based. Chamomile needs free-draining, moist soil, so shop-bought multipurpose compost is fine.

If you're growing chamomile from seed, it will need a bit of bottom heat to get it going. 'Treneague' doesn't come true from seed, but the species *C. nobile* does. You can also propagate by dividing plants in spring.

If you're creating a chamomile lawn, first, you lucky thing. Secondly, you'll need to work out how many plants to buy. As a rough guide, you'll need about 80–100 plants per 1m² (10¾sq ft), which means planting them about 15cm (6in) apart. If you're impatient, you can plant them closer together but that will require more plants and a bigger budget. Once the lawn is planted, try to keep off it for the first 3 months to let the plants establish themselves, and tread lightly for a year after that.

CARE

Trim chamomile in late summer to remove dead flower heads and the occasional ragged shoot. Water regularly – a soaking is better than watering little and often, but don't let the plant become waterlogged.

PESTS & DISEASES

There aren't any pest or diseases to worry about, though keep an eye out for aphids and mealybugs.

HARVEST & STORAGE

The flowers are ready to pick when the petals are flat or starting to fall back. As with all harvesting, the best time to collect the flowers is in the cool of the morning, just after any dew has dried but before the sun becomes too hot. Snip off the flowers and lay them on a sheet of paper or a drying tray for up to a couple of weeks. To test whether they're ready to be stored, try crumbling a flower; if it crumbles easily, transfer it to an airtight glass jar and store out of direct sunlight.

HOME REMEDIES

Chamomile tea is soothing and calming if you are prone to anxiety and is said to help relieve the symptoms of hay fever. The tea can also be used as a hair rinse to lighten blonde hair and to soothe itchy eyes (place a flannel soaked in the tea over the area).

For a relaxing bath, combine a handful of dried flowers with two handfuls of Epsom salts and add them to your bathwater. To make a lip scrub, infuse the flowers in sunflower oil, then add granulated sugar.

CULINARY USES

Add honey to chamomile tea to turn it into a refreshing cold drink to enjoy on long, hot summer days. If you make tea with fresh flowers, use twice the quantity you would use of dried flowers as drying intensifies the flavour.

Traditionally, chamomile's bitter taste was used to flavour herb beers. I haven't found a recipe to share with you, but it might be worth experimenting with the idea if you make your own craft beers.

❀ TOP TIPS

Try using chamomile tea to water seedlings – its fungicidal properties could help prevent the dreaded damping off.

Chamomile is meant to be a good bedfellow for basil as it increases the essential oils in basil plants, but I haven't tried this yet.

SWEETFERN

(COMPTONIA PEREGRINA)

Don't mistake this plant for a fern, as I did. Researching this book, I came across the sweetfern and thought it looked really appealing, with useful benefits for both the kitchen and the bathroom cabinet. I contacted a nurseryman to see if he had any stock and mistakenly referred to the plant as a "fern" – my error was rather sharply pointed out and I won't be making that mistake again. I ended up finding a bare-root plant in the United States.

This shrub was named after Henry Compton, Bishop of London (from 1675 to 1713), dendrologist and, rather fittingly, patron of botany. It's a really rather attractive addition to the garden and I love the spice aroma the leaves release when bruised.

GROW ◐ H 0.5-1.5M; S 0.5-1M

Sweetfern likes well-drained soil and some sunshine. In its native North America, it can be found in dry rocky clearings, pastures or open woodland, so it's pretty versatile. I grew my specimen in the glasshouse this year and it's thrived.

Looking at my small plant, it's hard to imagine that, left undisturbed, the sweetfern can rapidly form colonies. Given the lack of space in my plot, I think keeping it in a container is the best option.

CARE

Sweetfern is very easy to care for and doesn't require much in the way of watering, feeding or pruning. You can take root cuttings from an established plant.

PESTS & DISEASES

No real issues.

HARVEST & STORAGE

Pick leaves during the summer and autumn. The leaves can be used fresh or dried.

HOME REMEDIES

A tea made from the leaves and flowering tops can be used as a remedy for all manner of ailments, including diarrhoea, headaches and fever. I've learned that the leaves can also be used as a poultice for toothache and sprains, while an infusion, left to go cold, can help soothe poison ivy rash and stings.

The crushed leaves repel insects, and fresh leaves can be thrown onto a camp fire to keep mosquitoes away. The dried leaves can also be burnt as an incense.

CULINARY USES

Dried and powdered leaves can be used as a spice. The leaves make a pleasant-tasting tea.

FLOWERS & SHRUBS

GARDEN PINKS & CARNATIONS

(DIANTHUS SPP.)

I mentioned these gorgeous, old-fashioned flowers in the introduction to this book, so I won't repeat myself. Suffice to say, given their size, they're great for growing in containers on a windowsill or on the kitchen table, so in actual fact, they could feature in several chapters of this book. I chose this one, though, because I think they are a novel twist on shop-bought cut flowers. The next time you go to a friend's house for dinner, why not take a pot of pinks as a gift and suggest that it be used as a table centrepiece where everyone can appreciate the delicate flowers and breathe

in their clove scent? The pinks will keep on flowering for months, long after cut flowers would have been chucked in the bin, and you can encourage your friend to pick the blooms and use them to make syrups or crystallized flowers.

I wanted to grow *Dianthus* 'Mrs Sinkins' for this book. It is an old-fashioned variety with frilly white double flowers and a rich clove scent. It was incredibly popular in Victorian times. The story goes that it was supposed to be named after Queen Victoria, but the breeder, John Sinkins, decided to name it after his beloved wife instead. Being a bit disorganized myself, I left it too late to sow 'Mrs Sinkins' from seed. My attempts to source plug plants were unsuccessful and I had all but given up hope when I popped into my local independent garden centre, looking for containers, and found a tray of young 'Mrs Sinkins' plants. "Yay!"

'Mrs Sinkins' will flower modestly in the first year, but once the plant's established and settled it will flower prolifically year after year. If you like your blooms to be pert and tidy, this variety's probably not for you because it opens gradually and looks rather dishevelled. If you prefer uniformity, go for cottage-garden clove pinks (*D. caryophyllus*).

While researching this book, I came across a great website in the United States that specializes in old-fashioned heavily-scented cultivars. Next year, I'll be trying 'Charles Musgrave', which has a pretty white flower with a soft green centre, as well as a couple of cultivars with crazy star-shaped petals: the fringed pink 'Ambrosia', which looks incredible and was first listed nearly 200 years ago; and the fringed pink 'Rainbow Loveliness', which was a favourite of Christopher Lloyd, our national treasure and plantsman, who claimed it was one "that I would never want to be without". *Dianthus superbus* is also gorgeous and is purported to have some medicinal properties.

GROW ⬦ H 0.5-1M; W 0.1-0.5M

Find pinks a sunny spot and you'll get a great flush of flowers from midsummer to early autumn every year. I grew mine in containers, positioning them around the garden like a cut-flower display. I used small pots filled with shop-bought compost, even though they needed to be watered every day. If that sounds too onerous, you can plant them in the ground or in larger pots. Either way, make sure the soil doesn't hold water, especially in winter.

CARE

Deadhead the plants to encourage more flowers. Feed in spring. Take softwood cuttings of non-flowering shoots in summer or propagate by layering after flowering.

PESTS & DISEASES

Slugs can be a problem – stay vigilant.

HARVEST & STORAGE

Pick the flowers in the morning, just after they have bloomed and use fresh.

HOME REMEDIES

You can make a soothing tea with *D. caryophyllus* and *D. superbus* flowers to calm nerves and relieve stress.

CULINARY USES

I've made syrup with the flowers and used sugar to crystallize the flowers, which keep for 3 months. You can steep the flowers in wine, once you've removed the bitter white base, and you can flavour vinegar and fruit with the flowers, too.

ECHINACEA

(ECHINACEA SPP.)

Echinacea is known as the herbal remedy that can be taken pre-cold to boost our immune system in an effort to avoid or at least reduce cold symptoms. The plant from which this remedy is procured is gorgeous, with brightly coloured daisy-like blooms that flower from summer until late into the autumn. Echinacea comes in a variety of colours: from red and pink, and all the shades in between, to white, yellow, green, and even two-toned varieties. The central cone of the flower, which reminds me of a shuttlecock, is actually a mass of tiny fertile flowers that attract bees and butterflies, while the colourful petals simply serve to tempt the insects to come closer as they fly by. Make sure you're growing one of the four varieties that have medicinal properties: *Echinacea* spp., *E. angustifolia*, *E. purpurea* and *E. pallida*. My favourite species is *E. pallida* because it's more ethereal and seems to blend into the surrounding plants rather than dominating them.

GROW ⬢ H 1.5-2.5M; W 0.1-0.5M

Plant in a sunny open spot with well-drained soil. *E. pallida* takes a bit longer to get going than other types, but unlike *E. purpurea*, it will go the distance and behave more like a perennial than an annual.

CARE

If you haven't already picked the flowers, deadhead regularly to encourage new blooms. If you can, leave one or two flowers to go to seed for the birds and then cut these stems back in spring. Feed during the growing season and mulch to help conserve moisture.

PESTS & DISEASES

Aphids and leaf-hoppers.

HARVEST & STORAGE

Pick the flowers as soon as they bloom, cutting the stems above a pair of leaves. If drying, lay the leaves flat on a screen. In the autumn, you can harvest the root, digging up a small section and drying it, too. Store in an airtight jar out of direct sunlight.

HOME REMEDIES

A tea or tincture should be used at the first sign of a cold as it's thought not to help once the illness has taken hold. Generally, a tincture is preferable as it's more concentrated. To make echinacea tea, steep 2 teaspoons of either dried root or petals and leaves in 1 cup boiling water. A decoction (similar to a tea but steeped for longer) made using the dried root is also a useful remedy that boosts the immune system: add 1 teaspoon dried root and 1 cup boiling water to a saucepan, cover and simmer for up to 20 minutes, then strain and drink.

For a salve to treat minor wounds and insect bites, put 5 flowers and several leaves in a jar with just enough sunflower oil to cover and leave to infuse in the sunshine for about 4 weeks. (Alternatively, put the mixture in a bain marie and heat for several hours). Once the oil has infused, strain the oil into a heatproof bowl and add 14g (½oz) beeswax. Set the bowl over a bain marie and heat until the wax is melted. Pour the mixture into 55g (2oz) tins. The salve will keep for up to 1 year.

CULINARY USES

Echinacea petals make pretty decorations for home-baked cakes, soups and salads.

FLOWERS & SHRUBS

FUCHSIA

(FUCHSIA SPP.)

I didn't think I'd ever grow fuchsias as I find them brash and a bit fussy. However, last year I was filming for the BBC's *Gardeners' World* with one of its presenters, Nick Bailey, and he used the demure white variety *Fuchsia* 'Hawkshead' in a planting scheme for a small border in an urban front garden. This fuchsia had an upright bushy shape, which is useful in a border, and I particularly loved the way its masses of delicate white flowers sparkled out against the glossy green leaves. And it blooms from midsummer into autumn.

I have discovered that all fuchsia berries are edible, though some are more tasty than others. *Fuchsia magellanica* types, of which 'Hawkshead' is one, have the best flavour. I also came across a lilac fuchsia, *F. arborescens*, which is a quite different form of this typically showy species. Far more tender than other fuchsias, it is evergreen and produces sprays of elegant rose-pink flowers, followed by the delicious berries that give rise to its common name, Mexican blueberry. So, never say never. I'm now the proud grower of not one, but two fuchsias.

GROW ⬙ H 0.5–1M; W 0.1–0.5M

'Hawkshead' is a hardy type of fuchsia, so it's worth finding it a sheltered sunny or partially shady spot where it will be able to cope with all but the harshest of winters. *F. arborescens* is tender, so is best grown in a container where it can bask in the sunshine during summer and be brought indoors over winter. Both these fuchsias can be grown from seed or propagated with softwood cuttings.

CARE

To encourage the bushy habit of 'Hawkshead', pinch out the growing tips of each stem once it has about seven pairs of leaves. Water regularly and feed every month during the summer. Give it a trim in spring, ready for the growing season ahead. If there is a risk of severe frost, cover the plant with fleece.

PESTS & DISEASES

The elephant hawk-moth caterpillar loves fuchsias. This poses a dilemma because the pink and olive-green moths are beautiful but a large number of caterpillars can strip the stems of a fuchsia, causing mayhem. Ideally, pick off any caterpillars and find a patch of wild-growing rosebay willow herb for them to snack on instead. Also watch out for aphids, vine weevils and red spider mites in the glasshouse.

HARVEST & STORAGE

Harvest the berries when they are plump and smooth by twisting them off at the stem. A good tip is to freeze small quantities of the berries as you collect them, until you have enough to make jam.

HOME REMEDIES

The crushed flowers of *F. arborescens* can be used to soothe bites, scratches and grazes as the juice relieves itching and takes away the rednesss. They can also be used in water to relieve sunburn.

CULINARY USES

To make a delicious fuchsia jam, put 1 cup each of flowers and berries, 1 cup sugar, the juice of 1 lemon, 2 cups water and a peeled and chopped apple in a saucepan and simmer for 10 minutes. Let cool and then strain into a bowl. Add 2 tablespoons gelatine and leave the jam to set in the fridge.

SWEET WOODRUFF

(GALLIUM ODORATUM)

This is a fantastic plant for those awkward shady spots where little else will thrive. Even better, if you have a tree or a shrub in a border you can underplant it with sweet woodruff to make the most of an otherwise hard-to-fill space. Not only will the sweet woodruff brighten up bare soil, covering it with a mass of star-shaped leaves in early spring, followed by tiny white flowers, but also its sweet, grassy-scented leaves can be used in the kitchen and home. It's a good choice for a city garden because it isn't affected by pollution.

GROW ✌ H 0.1-0.5M; W 1-1.5M

Think shade – full or partial –as the leaves will become scorched in a sunny spot. Sow seed directly and try to recreate the plant's preferred natural habitat – leaf mould and shade from a tree will help germination, as does a snap of cold weather. In the right conditions, sweet woodruff is a fairly vigorous grower. You can stop the plants from spreading too quickly by keeping the soil dry – a good tip if you don't have a big border. Another solution would be to grow the plant in a container.

CARE

It is best to divide clumps of sweet woodruff in spring, though you can do this any time if you keep divisions moist until they're established. You can also take softwood cuttings after the plant has finished flowering, but they will need a bit of protection on a windowsill, in a cold frame or under a cloche until established.

PESTS & DISEASES

Nothing of note.

HARVEST & STORAGE

Sweet woodruff contains a fragrant chemical compound called coumarin, which produces the distinctive sweet smell of freshly mown hay as it dries. For optimal flavour and scent, harvest the leaves before the plants have flowered. To dry the leaves, tie them into bunches and hang them in a warm, dark place with low humidity.

HOME REMEDIES

In times gone by, sweet woodruff would have been strewn on floors to disguise unpleasant odours. These days it can be used as a subtle alternative to a lavender pillow or unfashionable pot pourri. I'm trying it out as a clothes-moth deterrent, too.

CULINARY USES

Depending on your taste buds, add a few leaves to boiling water for a grass-flavoured tea or use dried leaves for a stronger-tasting, relaxing sweet tea.

Sweet woodruff is a really popular plant in Germany, where it's called Waldmeister (forest master). The Germans have been using this plant for generations to make one of the nation's favourite punches, *Maibowle*. Fresh sprigs are steeped in sparkling white Riesling and drunk on the first of May. I've also read the same is popular in Alsace, though their aromatic version is called *Maitrank*.

Inspired by the Germans, who use it to make jams, jellies, brandy, beer, sausage, sherbets, sweets, soda and ice cream, I made a heavenly syrup. Steep about 100g (3½oz) washed sweet woodruff leaves and 3 sliced lemons in 2 litres (3½ pints) boiled sugar water for 1 day. Strain to remove the leaves and lemon and store in a sterilized flip-top bottle.

A word of warning: the stems contain a bitter milky substance so remove the leaves from the stem or place sprigs upside down in liquids to avoid the cut ends coming into contact with the liquid. It's best to use small amounts of sweet woodruff as too much can cause headaches and sickness.

HIBISCUS

(HIBISCUS SYRIACUS, H. ROSA-SINENSIS AND H. SABDARIFFA)

I was intrigued by the notion of drinking tea made from the huge colourful flowers of this exotic-looking plant. There are three main hibiscus species that are edible: *Hibiscus syriacus*, *H. rosa-sinensis* and *H. sabdariffa*. The common and hardy deciduous *Hibiscus syriacus* puts on a show of flowers from late summer into autumn, while the tender *H. rosa-sinensis* flowers from early summer into autumn, as long as it's given a fair amount of TLC. Blooms from both these species can be infused to make a mildly citrus-flavoured tea – it's lovely to serve friends with a fresh hibiscus flower to pop into a cup of hot water. When I first thought about growing this shrub for its flowers, I dreamt about *H. sabdariffa* (Roselle). You use the calyx (the sepals of the flower, which form a protective layer around the developing flower in bud) to flavour tea, syrups and vinegars with floral cranberry notes. It's difficult to get hold of a young plant in the UK, so I've grown it from seed. Like *H. rosa-sinensis*, it's tender, and it's trickier than *H. syriacus*, so needs to be raised indoors, in a glasshouse or on a south-facing windowsill.

GROW ✧ H 1-1.5M; W 0.5-1M

H. syriacus needs plenty of sun and well-drained soil. In the UK's climate, it will grow happily in a container or in the border. It's dormant until early summer but then rewards you by flowering well into the autumn. *H. rosa-sinensis* and *H. sabdariffa* need bright (but out of direct sunlight), humid conditions with plenty of ventilation and a temperature of 7°C (45°F), minimum. They can go outdoors in a hot summer, but need to be brought back inside before temperatures drop below 12°C (54°F).

CARE

Water and feed *H. syriacus* regularly to get it established and mulch it in autumn to provide extra protection from the cold. Remove any dead or damaged stems in spring. Propagate as softwood or semi-ripe cuttings in summer, putting these in a windowsill propagator. You can provide the right humid conditions for *H. rosa-sinensis* and *H. sabdariffa* by grouping plants together on a tray filled with clay pellets that are kept moist. Reduce regular watering and stop feeding altogether during winter. Prune in early spring and pinch out growing tips to create a bushier habit.

PESTS & DISEASES

H. syriacus is generally trouble free. Watch out for aphids, whitefly and red spider mites with *H. rosa-sinensis* and *H. sabdariffa*.

HARVEST & STORAGE

Pick the flowers of *H. syriacus* and *H. rosa-sinensis* to use fresh. To test whether the calyx of *H. sabdariffa* is ready to harvest, gently pull the flower, it will come away if it is ready. Once you've removed the calyx, poke out the pea-sized seed inside.

HOME REMEDIES

You can use the fresh or dried flowers of *H. syriacus* and *H. rosa-sinensis* and the fresh calyx of *H. sabdariffa* to make a tea that can help reduce high blood pressure and high cholesterol.

CULINARY USES

The fresh flowers of *H. syriacus* and *H. rosa-sinensis* and the fresh calyx of *H. sabdariffa* can be used to make a syrup using equal amounts of fresh flower or calyx, water and sugar. The calyx provides a stronger flavour, so you may need to add extra sugar.

SEA BUCKTHORN

(HIPPOPHAE RHAMNOIDES)

I'm excited to be growing this coastal-loving shrub. Its leaves are covered with a delicate silvery bloom that reminds me of the leaves of an olive tree, though they're more elongated in shape. While the flowers are small and, some might say, insignificant, the fruits are a gorgeous gaudy orange and are utterly divine. Although, so they should be, given the prickly battle you must endure to reach them. If you want a bountiful crop of berries, you will need to grow two plants (a male and a female) to ensure the flowers are pollinated.

GROW ⟋ H 4-8M; W 4-8M

Sea buckthorn is a survivor. Although it can do well growing in sand on exposed dunes, that's not to say it won't appreciate the finer things in life, like a bit of shade and normal soil. Choose the sunniest site possible. While it is often suggested as a hedge plant, it's doing very well in a container in my garden.

CARE

It quickly spreads by suckers in the wild, so much so that the RHS encourages care to be taken when discarding prunings. That said, if you're looking to bulk up your stocks or to grow plants as gifts for friends, take semi-ripe or hardwood cuttings.

PESTS & DISEASES

Nothing of note.

HARVEST & STORAGE

Given the spiny thorns, goggles and gloves are a sensible precaution when it's time to pick the berries in late autumn. Putting small branches in the freezer makes the berries easier to pick off the branch.

HOME REMEDIES

Sea buckthorn essential oil is widely used in skincare products as an anti-ageing treatment. It is also said to help soothe acne and minor wounds. Ideally, the oil should be extracted using fancy and expensive equipment. However, there are some good DIY methods you can try at home to make your own oil. Gather about 300g (10½oz) berries and wash and dry them. Put the berries in a jar and add 4 teaspoons alcohol, such as vodka. Seal the jar and let macerate for up to 6 days. Top up the jar with good-quality olive oil and seal again, stirring every day for 4 weeks. Eventually, you'll see a separate layer on the top of the liquid, which is the essential oil. Carefully pour off the oil, filtering it through a muslin cloth and transfer to small dark-coloured bottles.

CULINARY USES

Sea buckthorn berries are high in vitamin C. According to Ancient Greek mythology, Pegasus, the mythical winged stallion, loved these berries. And today, many horse supplements include extract of the seed or leaf to boost equine health.

As I mentioned in the introduction (page 4), I can vouch for the delicious flavour of sea buckthorn ice cream. Sea buckthorn juice is made by boiling the berries and then pressing the pulp through a sieve to release the juice. Admittedly, cooking the berries does release an unpleasant odour, but the resulting juice makes it worth having to open the windows in the depths of autumn. River Cottage forager, John Wright, suggests extracting the juice of 150g (5½oz) berries (as above) and then dissolving 75g (2¾oz) sugar in the hot juice before letting it cool. The resulting sugary sea buckthorn juice can be mixed with champagne to make a delicious cocktail.

FLOWERS & SHRUBS

JUNIPER

(JUNIPERUS SPP.)

This plant might test your commitment to growing botanicals – it did mine. I'm just not a fan of conifers. Although, if I'm being honest, my fear and loathing of conifers is largely directed at *C. leylandii*, or Leyland cypress, for obvious reasons – it's an ugly brute. However, setting to one side my rather predictable prejudice, the truth is there is plenty to recommend giving a conifer like juniper a place in your plot. It's evergreen for a start, and let's face it, any plant that will give you something to coo over when it's snowing and freezing outside deserves appreciation. It's also native to the UK, Europe and most of the Northern Hempishere, which is always a good thing as it means it's perfectly suited to our environment, and birds and moth caterpillars rely on it for food. Finally, juniper has aromatic stems and its berries are essential for making gin. Perhaps I should have started with that last point? Case closed, I think.

GROW ✦ H 0.1-0.5; W 1-1.5M

In general, junipers like plenty of sun and will tolerate poor, dry soils.

I spoke to a specialist conifer nursery to find out which type of juniper was the best one to grow. I did this because I'd read that the common variety can grow to an eventual height of 8m (26ft) and a spread of 4m (13ft), which is horribly reminiscent of leylandii and just not on for those of us with small gardens. It turns out there are various types of juniper that are relatively slow growing and can be pruned in spring to midsummer to keep them at the size you want.

- *Juniperus rigida* subsp. *Conferta* 'Schlager' is a low-growing plant. It has berries that are more bitter than other varieties, which could be good, depending on your taste buds.

- 'Green Carpet' is widely available and, as its name suggests, provides ground cover. It would make a lovely feature for a container or be useful as underplanting in a border.

- *Juniperus rigida* subsp. *conferta* has a cascading habit and would be a great specimen to cover a wall.

Do double-check that the type of juniper you choose is a culinary variety as, for example, *J. sabina* and *J. × pfitzeriana* are widely available in garden centres but aren't edible.

CARE

Prune lightly and often. If necessary, be bold in your pruning to keep the plant in check.

PESTS & DISEASES

Aphids, scale insects, webber moth caterpillars, twig blight and honey fungus.

HARVEST & STORAGE

I was fascinated to discover that juniper berries are actually a type of cone, the fleshy scales of which fuse together to form a berry. The berries are usually harvested in the autumn when fully ripe, which can take up to 2 years. Berries should be dried for later use.

HOME REMEDIES

A tea made from the dried berries can help digestion, urinary tract infections and kidney stones. The berries produce an oil, which can be used to aid respiratory and digestive problems. A decoction of the branches can be used as an anti-dandruff shampoo and fresh or dried juniper branches also make a good insect repellent.

CULINARY USES

As I've already mentioned, juniper berries are used to flavour gin (see page 40). The ripe black berries can also be used in dishes like sauerkraut, stuffings and pâtés. The seeds can be roasted to create a coffee substitute – I haven't tried this yet, but intend to – and you can make a spicy gin-like tea from the berries and leaves.

ENGLISH LAVENDER

(LAVANDULA ANGUSTIFOLIA)

I must confess, my heart used to sink a little at the mention of a lavender-flavoured cake or biscuit. Rather than adding a delicate floral note, it always overpowered the food and made me think of my granny's drawers (the furniture kind, not underwear), which wasn't particularly appetizing. However, as with all things in life, it pays to keep an open mind. Nowadays, I'm a bit of a lavender fan, though this change of heart is largely down to the miraculous medicinal benefits of lavender rather than its culinary uses.

For over a year my sleeping patterns were all over the place. Keen to try to stay happy and healthy, I decided to take getting a decent night's sleep seriously. I found a lavender spray for my pillow and a lavender-scented tincture to rub on my wrists. Lavender is well known for its calming and relaxing qualities and I found that it really did help. The effects weren't immediate. For a month or so I still had broken nights of sleep, but using the spray and tincture allowed me to get back to sleep quickly and I found I was sleeping for longer periods of time.

Inspired by the success of lavender as a herbal remedy, I decided to try using lavender in recipes, too. Eating to further improve my sleep patterns appealed to both the piglet and sloth in me. I discovered lots of different ways to use this herb to flavour food, over and above the dreaded (to me, anyway) lavender shortbread. Unsurprisingly, when it comes to using lavender as an ingredient, I remain convinced that less is definitely more.

While all English lavender is edible, French lavender (*Lavandula stoechas*) isn't. For intensity of flavour there are a few cultivars that stand out from the rest. I went for *L. angustifolia* 'Melissa Lilac' and *L. × intermedia* 'Grosso', in my garden, which are the varieties that top chefs prefer to use. If it's good enough for them…

GROW ◈ H 0.5-1M; W 0.5-1M

Lavender is nice and easy to grow. Coming from hot Mediterranean countries, it really doesn't need much in the way of watering or rich soil. In fact, the poorer and more free-draining the soil, the better. Sow from seed in early spring in pots in an unheated greenhouse. If you're planting in clay, or creating a container display, don't be shy with the horticultural grit, you'll need to add plenty to open up the soil's structure.

If you don't have a border or room for many containers, lavender is perfectly suited to planting in gravel. Actually, it's a great way to utilize space in a front yard, especially when the tiny strip of a "garden" has been covered with shale. You can soften the expanse of hard landscaping by planting lavender in the ground, making sure there's plenty of drainage so that the roots don't sit in wet, boggy soil. If, like me, you have a layer of membrane to suppress weeds, simply scrape off the top layer of gravel and cut an X-shape in the fabric. Fold back the four cut pieces of fabric to reveal the soil underneath and remove the fabric flaps. Dig a hole a

CONTINUED…

FLOWERS & SHRUBS

LAVENDER CONTINUED...

little larger than the size of the pot the lavender is in, add plenty of horticultural grit, if needed, remove the lavender from its pot and plant it. Back-fill the hole with soil and firm down, then carefully re-cover the soil with the shale and water the lavender well.

CARE

The trick to having a great-looking lavender bush is all in your chosen method of pruning. There's lots of discussion about whether you should prune straight after flowering or wait until the following spring, and whether you should give lavender a short-back-and-sides before the weather starts hotting up. My experience proves that cutting it back in summer, when the flowers have faded, produces happy, healthy plants the following season. Also, if you cut the stems back by about one-third in early autumn, the new shoots that appear at the base of the plant have time to harden off before winter sets in.

PESTS & DISEASES

Happily, there are no pests or diseases to worry about. You might find cuckoo spit (a white frothy liquid secreted by froghopper larvae) on the plant in late spring and summer, but it can be washed off with a hose.

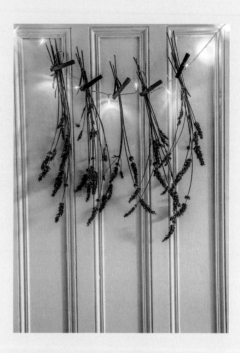

HARVEST & STORAGE

Using garden shears, trim the long green stems, making sure not to cut the wiry and woody branches and the leaves at the crown of the plant. A lovely tip I picked up is to lightly brush the top of the plant to scare away any bees or bugs before harvesting the stems.

You can use lavender fresh or dry it for later use. Hanging a bouquet of lavender upside-down to dry will draw the essential oils down into the flower buds. Once it is really dry, it should be stored in a cool, dark place so it doesn't go mouldy. I've read that culinary lavender, stored properly in an airtight container, will stay flavourful and fragrant for up to 3 years, but I'm currently only on year one so can't guarantee that.

I like to peg small bunches of lavender along a string of lights in my living room. It looks really pretty and fills the room with a nice scent, too.

HOME REMEDIES

Lavender has incredible healing properties. The key to using lavender is extracting its essential oil. You can do this using the simple technique on page 74.

You can use lavender essential oil on mild burns (after first running the burn under the cold tap). For a very soothing balm, mix 10 drops of lavender oil with about 60g (about ¼ cup) aloe vera gel.

You can also use lavender oil to repel insects, soothe insect bites, relieve chapped lips and cold sores, reduce dandruff (rub directly on your scalp), alleviate hay fever symptoms (rub the oil in the palm of your hands and then deeply inhale), and, of course, help you to sleep and relax. My two favourite remedies are to place a drop of lavender oil on your navel to calm motion sickness and to wrap an ice cube in a tissue with a drop of lavender oil on it and place it on your top lip to help stop a nose bleed.

For a simple and cheap alternative to a room fragrance, scatter some dried lavender buds on your carpet before using the vacuum cleaner.

CULINARY USES

I love the idea of using lavender stems, which have a delicious sweet-savoury flavour, to stir drinks or as a skewer for kebabs.

Lavender lemonade is an inspired twist on a traditional favourite, and it's easy to make. Put 60g (2¼oz) dried lavender in a bowl, pour over 600ml (1 pint) boiling water and let steep for 10 minutes before straining. You can add this lavender infusion to the usual combination of sugar, lemon and water to make lemonade (150g/5½oz sugar, the juice of 8 lemons and enough cold water to fill a 2.4-litre/ 4-pint pitcher). Don't forget to add plenty of ice before serving.

To make lavender syrup, put 3 tablespoons dried lavender, 150g (5½oz) sugar and 450ml (16fl oz)

water in a saucepan and bring to the boil to dissolve the sugar, then reduce the heat and simmer for 15 minutes. Strain the syrup and pour into a sterilized bottle.

You can also infuse fresh flowers in salt. Using about one part flowers (ensure they are absolutely dry) to ten parts coarse sea salt, mix the flowers and salt together and then grind in a spice mill or with a pestle and mortar.

DYNAMIC DUO

Lavender plants and grape vines are a perfect pairing. When planted together, the lavender helps ward off bugs and viruses.

HONEYSUCKLE

(LONICERA PERICLYMENUM)

I wanted to include the UK's native wild honeysuckle in this book because as a child I loved to pick the individual flowers and suck the ends to get a sweet sugary hit from the nectar. Honeysuckle's nectar is like a natural alternative to a square or two of chocolate when you're craving something sweet. For that reason alone, I think we should all grow honeysuckle in our gardens. I also wanted to include this plant for its delicious honey fragrance and the fact that, as a climber, it offers a floriferous disguise for ugly walls or unsightly spots. Birds love it, too, seeking refuge in its dense leaves and gorging on its berries.

I came across a beautiful honeysuckle called 'Scentsation' when I was visiting one of the RHS Flower Shows, researching stories for the television programme I work on. I couldn't have been more excited to find this particular cultivar. It was discovered in a hedgerow in the county in which I grew up, and the nursery's stand even featured a gorgeous hand-crafted, traditional-style oak fence that was sourced from an oak tree that grew in the village I'd lived in for over 20 years. 'Scentsation' has pretty flowers, it's thought to be the most scented *Lonicera periclymenum* and it's a fast grower, but to be honest, I was convinced it was the variety for me before I knew any of that. This was one of many serendipitous moments I had during the research for this book and I'm delighted to share it with you.

GROW ✆ H: 4-8M; W 1.5-2.5M

This hardy evergreen climber is fairly happy to romp away if you keep its roots cool and in the shade – the rest of the plant can bask in the sun. This honeysuckle does best in full sun or semi-shade in well-drained soil. If, like me, you're going to plant it in a container, make sure you add a good amount of horticultural grit.

CARE

Keep watered during dry spells and mulch with well-rotted organic matter. Trim lightly after flowering to prevent the plant becoming leggy.

PESTS & DISEASES

Powdery mildew.

HARVEST & STORAGE

This honeysuckle flowers from midsummer until early autumn, so gather the flowers a cup full at a time. Ideally, leave a few flowers on the plant as they will be replaced by red berries, which the birds will like to eat. Be warned: the berries are not for human consumption as they're poisonous.

HOME REMEDIES

A tea made from the leaves and flowers, which are rich in salicylic acid, may relieve headaches, colds, flu, fever, pain, arthritis and rheumatism. The tea can also be used as a mouthwash or gargle to treat ulcers and to soothe dry, scratchy throats.

CULINARY USES

The flowers can be transformed into a wonderful syrup that can be added to vinaigrettes and jellies, as well as being an exciting addition to fizzy water and brandy cocktails. Use honeysuckle-infused water to make refreshing sorbets, cordials and conserves.

BERGAMOT

(MONARDA SPP.)

It is a common misconception that this herb is used to flavour Earl Grey tea; it's actually the citrus bergamot that's used in the tea. This plant is called bergamot because some varieties smell like the citrus fruit.

This gorgeous group of plants looks great grown in a container or a border. I've grown two varieties in my Tetris border (see page 32) – the white *Monarda* 'Schneewittchen' and the purple *M.* 'Prärienacht' – because not only do the bees, butterflies and other beneficial insects love them, but also they flower all summer long, are easy to grow and can be used to make a delicious tea. I've also planted *M. citriodora*, otherwise known as lemon mint (though it's not a member of the mint family), together with lemon verbena (see page 106) and Indian mint (see page 138), where it looks beautiful and provides a citrus fiesta.

GROW ⬡ H 0.5-1M; W 0.1-0.5M

Bergamot is a sun-worshipper, though light shade is acceptable for this perennial. It won't thank you if it sits in very wet or very dry soil.

CARE

Deadhead to encourage flowering and, if you want the blooms to extend into late summer, cut back in late spring (otherwise known as the "Chelsea Chop", see page 142). I gave 'Schneewittchen' the Chelsea Chop so that when the nepeta fades in early autumn the bergamot will pick up the flowering baton and provide a splash of colour into mid-autumn. Once the flowers fade in autumn, cut the plant back to the ground. Sow seeds or divide in spring.

PESTS & DISEASES

Powdery mildew in dry conditions. (My 'Prärienacht' suffered from powdery mildew towards the end of the long, hot summer, so I removed the leaves and burned them rather than adding to the compost bin – obviously, I didn't harvest any unhealthy leaves.)

HARVEST & STORAGE

Pick the leaves to use fresh or dry stems and then strip the leaves and blossoms from the stems and store in an airtight glass jar.

HOME REMEDIES

Bergamot tea can be left to go cold and then used to soothe a sore throat. You can squeeze juice from the leaves onto cuts and grazes to help heal them.

CULINARY USES

You can make a bergamot jelly by using a tea made from the petals and then adding sugar and pectin. Rather fittingly, because bergamot is also known as bee balm, the jelly has a honey taste with a hint of mint.

FLOWERS & SHRUBS

SCENTED-LEAVED PELARGONIUMS

(PELARGONIUM SPP.)

My mum loves growing the common red and white pelargoniums (commonly known as geraniums, but not to be confused with hardy geraniums). She buys them every year for her garden as a reminder of family holidays in the Mediterranean. Without being rude to my mum, it was the rather more demure and sophisticated *Pelargonium* 'Lord Bute' that persuaded me to grow pelargoniums.

While 'Lord Bute' is a sensational plant with blackish-purple flowers, I stick to growing scented-leaved pelargoniums for the obvious reason that they allow me to introduce an array of delicious flavours to food. The plant's scent glands are at the base of its leaf hairs, so crushing the leaves releases the scent. Scented-leaved pelargoniums tend to have smaller flowers than other types of pelargonium, but they're prolific flowerers, so you'll still get plenty of colour in addition to the fragrant leaves that come in a variety of different sizes, shapes and colours.

GROW ✦ H 0.1-0.5M; W 0.1-0.5M

While most types of scented-leaved pelargonium are happy to bask in the sun, a bit of shade is often appreciated. Make sure the soil isn't too rich as this can reduce the strength of the plant's fragrance.

If growing indoors or under glass, grow in full light, shaded from the scorching midday sun. If you grow them inside, they'll need bright light to stop them getting leggy. If they start to look straggly, give them a light prune to encourage a bushier shape.

CARE

Pelargoniums respond very well to regular feeds of high potash during the growing season. Pinch back pelargoniums in spring or early summer to encourage further branching. Tall, vigorously growing cultivars can be trained on canes to form a pillar.

If grown in pots, water sparingly every few days, feed once a week during the growing season, cut plants back by two-thirds during the winter and keep them almost dry. If grown in borders, pelargoniums will need to be lifted and overwintered indoors.

These plants propagate easily from cuttings and can be grown as decorative pot plants inside or outside in the summer. Take cuttings when they begin to shoot in spring.

PESTS & DISEASES

Vine weevil, mealybugs, whitefly, grey mould and rust.

HARVEST & STORAGE

Pick young leaves and flowers just as they bloom and use fresh.

HOME REMEDIES

Bruise fresh leaves and rub them on insect bites or scratches. The flowers and leaves can be used to make a tea that can help with anxiety and soothe the digestive system. Rose-scented geraniums (*Pelargonium graveolens*) are said to help put you in a better mood.

CULINARY USES

Finely chopped leaves can be used to make a flavoured butter or added to savoury doughs, especially for scones. The flowers can be used for decoration or to make pretty ice cubes. To make a pelargonium-scented sugar, gently bruise some fresh leaves, arrange them in a jar between layers of sugar and let stand somewhere warm for up to 4 weeks. The scented sugar can be used in baking or to make jellies. The fresh leaves can also be infused in vinegar or added to sorbets and ice creams for a few weeks to impart their delicate flavour.

In addition to the rose-scented geranium, here's my pick of pelargoniums with interesting fragrances that will enhance your homecooked dishes:

- 'Charity' has a bushy habit and a spicy orange scent.
- 'Lady Scarborough' is upright and slow-growing, and it smells of sherbet.
- 'Mabel Grey' is tall and upright with lemon-scented leaves.
- 'Pink Capricorn' has a trailing habit and its leaves have a lemon-rose fragrance.
- 'Prince of Orange' is bushy and orange-scented.
- 'Radula Rosea' has a spreading habit and a pungent, spicy scent.
- 'Torrento' has a bushy habit and a ginger scent.
- 'Welling' has a bushy habit and a spiced citrus scent.

❀ TOP TIP

In the same way that you can make a liquid feed with comfrey leaves (see page 96), you can make a natural plant booster with equal parts of geranium leaves and comfrey leaves.

ROSE

(ROSA SPP.)

According to annual surveys commissioned by the horticultural industry and gardening magazines, roses are among the most popular flowers to be grown. I'd wager that this preference belongs to a slightly older demographic. I realize that could be a controversial opinion, but when I think about my friends' gardens, roses simply aren't a feature.

While most of us might not complain if we were given a bunch of roses by our significant other (although, at the risk of sounding picky, if they're not in season and homegrown, I'd prefer something more wild and less obvious), when it comes to growing these old-fashioned favourites, I think they're quite low down on the wish list for younger gardeners. This may be because younger generations associate roses with their grandparents, who grew individual scraggly bush roses in funny isolated island borders in the 1970s. I imagine there's a perception that roses need lots of space. And then there's the issue of cost – they're not the cheapest plants to buy.

That said, I urge you to find space for roses in your garden. From a botanical point of view, roses are complete all-rounders and their flowers and rosehips can be used medicinally, in the kitchen and for beauty treatments. In other words, there's definitely something for everyone.

'Harlow Carr', 'Gertrude Jekyll' and 'Susan Williams-Ellis' are among my favourite of the strongly scented types of roses. In the past I've grown the repeat flowering climbing white rose 'Madame Alfred Carrière', and I would recommend it. It's a good choice if space is tight because you can trail it up and along walls or trellis, and it provides plenty of seasonal interest.

For my botanical garden, I chose a truly gorgeous rose: 'Chartreuse de Parme'. It's a modern hybrid tea rose that has been bred for long repeat flowering as well as disease resistance and, most importantly, an incredible scent that reminds me of Turkish Delight. I figured, if you're going to use a rose for face creams, decorations or to flavour drinks, go for a truly delicious scent. I also grow the common *Rosa rugosa* because it produces huge rosehips that can be used to make a fragrant syrup, fruit leather and tea.

CONTINUED...

FLOWERS & SHRUBS

ROSE CONTINUED...

GROW ✿ H 1–2M; W 1–2M

Roses are a surprisingly versatile group of plants. Most need at least four hours of sunlight per day, though there are types that are fine against a north-facing wall in the shade. Avoid exposed and windy sites and give your roses heavy soil if you can – clay is best. If you're growing a rose in a container, add plenty of organic matter to shop-bought compost.

You can buy roses as bare-root plants in autumn and spring. Bare-root plants are cheaper than pot-grown alternatives, but pot-grown roses are available year round. Before planting, soak the bare-root plant or pot-grown plant in its pot in water. To plant, dig a hole and add plenty of organic matter, then sprinkle some mycorrhizal fungi powder on the roots to encourage healthy growth, plant in the ground, making sure that the grafting bud on the stem is just below the surface of the soil, and water well.

CARE

Deadhead in summer after flowering and prune in winter. Water well until the plant is established. Feed every fortnight during the growing season and mulch each spring.

PESTS & DISEASES

Powdery mildew, blackspot and rust can be an issue for roses, while aphids, blackfly, leaf-hoppers and sawfly are troublesome pests. However, disease-resistant rose varieties help combat these problems.

HARVEST & STORAGE

Pick flowers in the morning, as soon as the sun has dried any dew on the petals. Ideally, you'll want to be able to harvest both the flowers and rosehips, so pluck the petals, rather than cutting the flower, and leave the centre of the flower intact to ripen. The rosehips will be ready to pick after the first frosts, when they're still bright and rosy red. Remove the stems and blossom ends from the rosehips and use fresh or dry.

To dry rose petals, lay them on a screen in the shade (direct sun will make them fade) and leave outdoors to dry. Alternatively, use a dehydrator on its lowest heat. Store the petals in a glass jar out of direct light.

CULINARY USES

You can make tea with dried rose petals. The fresh petals can be used to infuse white wine or apple cider vinegar: put 2 cups fresh rose petals and 1 litre (1¾ pints) white wine or cider vinegar in a sterilized glass jar and let infuse for a month in a

---

MY TOP THREE ROSES FOR BEAUTY PRODUCTS THAT ARE ALSO EDIBLE, SO DELICIOUS AS A TEA

Rosa × damascene is an ancient shrub rose. It has spring-flowering pink flowers with a heavy scent and hardly any thorns. Its petals can be used to make rosewater and perfume.

Rosa × centifolia is rather inappropriately called the cabbage rose. I think we can assume that's because of the beautiful clusters of pink petals rather than its fragrance.

Rosa gallica is another old rose variety, known as the apothecary rose. It's more of a dog rose with an open flower as opposed to a tight cluster of petals. It produces great rosehips in autumn.

cool, dark place. Strain the mixture and transfer to sterilized bottles or jars. The rose vinegar will keep for up to 1 year.

Rosehip syrup is divine. It's worth straining twice, though, to remove those tiny hairs from the rosehips, which can be an irritant.

HOME REMEDIES

Rose petals can be used to make very pretty scrubs, creams and waters. They're good for your skin, too. I've included a few recipes below, but you can find lots more online, so have a look and see which ones take your fancy (also see pages 45–46).

SIMPLE SUGAR SCRUB

Put 1 cup dried rose petals in a food processor or blender and pulse until they are small flakes. Transfer to a bowl, add 2 cups (360g/12½oz) sugar and mix well. Add 2 cups (450ml/16fl oz) sweet almond oil and several drops of rose oil and stir to combine. If you prefer, you can replace the sugar with a similar quantity of ground oats. The scrub will keep for up to 1 month in an airtight container. When you are ready to use the scrub, scoop out a quantity (use a spoon, don't scoop it out directly with wet hands) and apply it to your skin.

REJUVENATING ROSEWATER

This is the quickest and easiest method I've found for making rosewater: put 1 cup rose petals into a glass jar and pack down, then cover with 2 cups boiling water and let steep until the water is cool. Strain the mixture, squeezing the petals to extract all the liquid. Store the rosewater in an airtight jar in the refrigerator for up to 2 weeks.

REFRESHING ROSE TONER

In a bowl, mix together 175ml (6fl oz) witch hazel and 6 drops glycerin to 250ml (9fl oz) rosewater. Store in an airtight jar in the refrigerator for up to 2 weeks.

ROSE-A-LUSCIOUS LIP BALM

Put 120ml (4fl oz) sweet almond oil and 2 tablespoons dried rose petals in a saucepan, bring to the boil and then immediately remove from the heat and let cool overnight. Strain the rose oil into a heatproof glass bowl and add 5 tablespoons grated beeswax and 1 teaspoon honey. Set the bowl over a saucepan of simmering water, making sure the base of the bowl doesn't touch the water, and heat until the rose oil has melted, then add the liquid from 2 vitamin E capsules and stir to combine. Transfer the mixture to small pots and seal. The lip balm will keep for up to 2 months.

DWARF ELDER

(SAMBUCUS NIGRA 'INSTANT KARMA')

Elder was one of the first botanicals my editor mentioned for the book. We felt that the elderflowers and berries were the right fit for the list: delicious, easy to use in a variety of different ways and a real asset to the botanical-lover's garden. However, the big issue was, well, the plant's size. An elder tree just isn't suited to small spaces or compact containers. Reluctantly, I pushed the elder to the bottom of the list. That is, until I found *Sambucus nigra* 'Instant Karma', which has a compact habit and can be grown in a decent-sized container. Compared to its larger cousins, this dwarf variety reaches about 2.5m (8¼ft) tall and can be curtailed easily with judicious pruning. I was delighted to find that 'Instant Karma' is variegated and looks really pretty, even without its trademark flowers and berries. Bingo!

GROW ☙ H 2-3M; Q 0.05-1M

The dwarf elder is best grown in the ground, if possible, and actually benefits from its roots being roughly handled when it's planted. However, if a container is your only option, go for the largest elder your budget and garden can cope with. It will be happy in full sun or partial shade and adapts to wet or dry soils. The dwarf elder can be trained as a small tree or large shrub or cut back as a perennial.

CARE

Cut back after flowering. Take softwood cuttings in early summer or hardwood cuttings in winter.

PESTS & DISEASES

Disease resistant and drought tolerant.

HARVEST & STORAGE

Elderflowers are ready to harvest in early summer. They're best picked on a warm, dry, sunny day when the buds are newly open. Gently shake the blossom to remove any insects.

Elderberries come in the autumn, but only if you've left some flowers on the plant. Do not eat any other part of the elder tree as the leaves are poisonous (although they can be used to make an infused oil to use in balms to help bruises and sprains).

HOME REMEDIES

For an oil that's gentle on the skin and can be used to make salves, infuse one part elderflower in three parts oil (a combination of olive and grapeseed oil is ideal) and leave for 3 weeks.

A tea made with dried elderflowers can help the body reduce inflammation and release toxins by increasing perspiration, making it a good option for blocked-up noses, sore throats and winter colds. Is also said to reduce the symptoms of hay fever if taken a few months prior to the hay-fever season.

CULINARY USES

We all know about elderflower cordial and elderflower champagne, but this year I was tempted to bypass the bubbles and go straight for a vodka-based liqueur. Simply combine about 20 flower heads, 125g (4½oz) sugar (or a few leaves of stevia), the juice of 1 lemon and 1 litre (1¾ pints) vodka in a sterilized jar and let infuse for a couple of months, shaking the contents every day for the first 2 weeks.

A delicious syrup or liqueur made from elderberries can be used to strengthen immunity during winter.

BURNET

(SANGUISORBA SPP.)

I chose two burnets for my botanical garden: salad burnet (*Sanguisorba minor*, now *Poterium sanguisorba*) to grow in containers and great burnet (*S. officinalis*) for my Tetris border (see page 32).

I love the blueish-green rosettes of salad burnet's scalloped leaves, which, as an added bonus, have a delicious cucumber flavour and scent. When I was planning my window boxes, this evergreen plant seemed a great choice because I'd be able to enjoy its lush foliage all year round. Salad burnet's new growth reaches up to 50cm (1½ft) in height, while its elegant, spindly flower stems are taller still. Grown in a window box, it acts like a living net curtain without blocking out the light in the way material might. Salad burnet's flowers are like crazy balls from which sprout little pink buds that remind me of coral. I'm not surprised that butterflies go wild for them. If you're growing salad burnet in the ground, pop it at the front of a border – it's only its flower stems that get tall so it won't swamp neighbouring plants.

The flowers of great burnet are less quirky but perfect for providing splashes of deep red all over a border. I was sad not to be able to use *Verbena bonariensis* in my garden this year (it didn't cut the botanical criteria), but I soon forgot my disappointment thanks to great burnet, which lifts a planting scheme in a similar way. Its leaves are like bigger versions of salad burnet, though they don't have the same juicy cucumber flavour.

GROW ◇ H 1-1.5M; W 0.1-0.5M

Both burnets are usually found in grassland, which means they ideally love chalky, dry soil. Having said that, I found they grew perfectly well in shop-bought compost. Sow seeds of both in spring or autumn. Burnets send down long taproots. If the plants outgrow their pots or become congested in a border, divide them in spring and autumn too.

CARE

You can cut this plant back after flowering, though I left the seedheads on my plants to create a more interesting view from the window during the winter.

PESTS & DISEASES

None to mention.

HARVEST & STORAGE

For salad burnet, pick the leaves regularly, though keep in mind that the plant may not flower if you're picking lots of leaves all the time. For great burnet, harvest the leaves before flowering.

HOME REMEDIES

The name *Sanguisorba* comes from the Latin *sanguis*, meaning "blood", and *sorbeo*, meaning "absorbing", which might explain why soldiers in the Middle Ages were said to have drunk infusions of this plant in the hope their wounds wouldn't bleed too much. These days, burnet is largely cultivated for its medicinal uses. Tea made from the dried leaves of great burnet can be used as a mouthwash or a gargle for sore throats. Water infused with the fresh leaves of either plant can be used to soothe sunburn and eczema and calm the bowels.

CULINARY USES

In Elizabethan times, salad burnet was thought to "yeeldeth a certain grace in the drinking" when the herb was added to wine. I've tried it and I think it's better in spritzers and soft drinks like lemonade. A few sprigs of leaves can be used to flavour beer (think of it as a beer bouquet garni) and vinegar.

Great burnet flowers can be used to make wine. I found a great recipe, originally from the *Nottingham Evening Post* in 1935, for a wine that becomes quite like port if you store it for a few months. Rather confusingly, both *S. minor* and *S. officinalis* can be called salad burnet. The recipe refers to salad burnet but I think they might have meant great burnet because my research suggests that salad burnet leaves are only added to wine as a garnish.

For burnet wine, put 2.25 litres (2 quarts) great burnet flowers, pressed down, and 1.8kg (4lb) sugar in a large saucepan with 4.5 litres (1 gallon) boiling water, then add the juice of 2 oranges and 2 lemons, a few cloves and 25g (1oz) crushed fresh root ginger (suspended in the liquor in a muslin bag). When the liquor is cool, add a piece of toast spread with 25g (1oz) yeast and let the mixture stand for 7 days, stirring daily. Transfer to a cask and bung lightly. When fermentation has ceased, cork firmly: bottle after 3 months.

COMFREY

(SYMPHYTUM OFFICINALE)

If you're keen to garden organically – and why wouldn't you want to do so if you're eating what you're growing? – comfrey is your friend; its leaves are rich with nitrogen, phosphorus and potassium (three times as much of the latter as you'll find in farmyard manure). This triumvirate of nutrients is vital for plant health and growth. Just as you can make teas to boost your own health and vitality, so you can make a liquid feed for plants using comfrey leaves. If you're stuck for space, I'll be honest, growing comfrey might not be at the top of your list. However, you could try teaming up with your neighbours or friends to find a disused space where you could grow a pot and share the spoils of the liquid fertilizer once it's made. You could also keep an eye out for comfrey growing in the wild. Russian comfrey (*Symphytum* x *uplandicum*) has an even higher nutrient content than wild comfrey (*Cynoglossum virginianum*); its leaves can be harvested several times during the growing season and it doesn't produce as many seeds, so it won't take over a border.

GROW ✧ H 0.5-1M; W 0.5-1M

Comfrey is happy in most soils and likes sunshine. Comfrey is considered by some to be too vigorous to grow in a pot, but I've only ever grown it in good-sized containers (about 30cm/12in wide).

CARE

Remove the flower stem in the first season to help the plant bulk up and produce plenty of leaves the following year. If you have grass cuttings, or know someone who does, add a few handfuls of grass around the base of the plant every now and then to encourage even more leaf growth. Alternatively, you could mulch the plant with well-rotted manure.

PESTS & DISEASES

Slugs.

HARVEST & STORAGE

To make a comfrey liquid feed, put 1kg (2lb 4 oz) comfrey leaves in a large bucket of water and let it steep for 4–6 weeks – it will produce a marvellous, if somewhat smelly, liquid. Alternatively, you can make a concentrate without using water, which is the method I prefer as it takes up less space and the resulting liquid is less pungent. To do this, simply pack as many comfrey leaves as you can into a plastic bottle, replace the lid and puncture a hole in the top of the lid. Turn the bottle upside down and hang it above a container to collect the liquid feed. As the leaves decay, a highly concentrated liquid will drip out of the bottle. To use the liquid feed, add about 1 part water to 10 parts concentrate.

HOME REMEDIES

For centuries, comfrey has been used as a tea to help soothe coughs and as a poultice to help heal minor cuts and scrapes. In recent years, there has been some discussion about comfrey causing liver disease, so I would advise using it only externally. To make a poultice, take a couple of leaves and remove the hairs on them by rubbing the leaves together, then wrap the leaves around a wound and apply pressure to help soothe and heal.

CULINARY USES

Comfrey is not for eating!

NASTURTIUM

(TROPAEOLUM MAJUS)

Nasturtiums are one of those brilliant plants that cover a multitude of sins. They're happy to self-seed and grow in all but the tiniest crevice or crack, hiding all manner of unsightly areas with their lush green leaves and bright, bold flowers. There are some gorgeous colours available, from the deep-red 'Black Velvet' to the pale cream 'Milkmaid', and you can choose from a climbing, trailing or compact habit. Whatever space you have, there's a nasturtium to fill it.

GROW ⬵ H 1.5-2.5M; W 1.5-2.5M

Sow seeds directly in the ground or in a container in spring and you'll be enjoying a mass of flowers from summer until autumn. While nasturtiums are said to like sunny spots in soil with good drainage, to be honest, I think these little tough nuts would have a go at growing anywhere.

CARE

Nasturtiums don't need too much in the way of care. Don't feed them, otherwise you'll just get leaves and very few flowers. Similarly, don't overwater – keep watering to a minimum unless they're in a container.

PESTS & DISEASES

Slugs and snails.

HARVEST & STORAGE

Pick flowers early in the morning, snipping off and discarding the bitter-tasting base. The leaves and young green seedpods are edible.

HOME REMEDIES

Given the natural antibiotic properties of the leaves, chewing one leaf per hour at the first sign of a sore throat can help soothe and reduce the infection.

For hair loss, make an infusion by putting 1 cup nasturtium flowers and 1 litre (1¾ pints) water in a saucepan, then cover with a lid and simmer for 15 minutes. Strain, let it cool and store in an airtight container. Massage the infusion into the scalp, rinse your hair and repeat as required.

CULINARY USES

You can pickle young seeds and use them like mock capers. Young leaves are tasty in salads – the more mature the leaf, the stronger the flavour– and the flowers provide a nice spicy hit.

VIOLA

(VIOLA CORNUTA, V. TRICOLOR, V. × WITTROCKIANA & V. ODORATA)

These dainty little scented plants are absolutely perfect for adding colour to container displays, window boxes and dull spots in the garden. Flowering from spring until autumn, the more diminutive types of viola, which are the best ones to use in the kitchen, are an easy way to add a flourish to homemade salads and cakes. I'm all for packing them into your growing space because the more plants you have, the more liberal you can be when it comes to using them.

I was interested to find out more about violas because of the Parma violets sweets; I wondered whether I could recreate that flavour myself. *Viola odorata*, the wood violet, is the highly scented viola that the scent for the sweets is based on. It flowers from as early as late winter until early summer and can continue to flower, though less enthusiastically, until the autumn.

GROW ⬡ H 0.1–0.5M; W 0.1–0.5M

According to Wildegoose Nursery, in Shropshire, UK, the key to having a dazzling display of violas is to give the plants plenty of depth for their roots to spread into; if you're growing violas in a container, choose one that's at least 30cm (12in) deep. Violas like moist but well-drained soil. Add plenty of organic matter to the soil prior to planting in the ground. Violas aren't fussy about a bit of shade. Sow seeds in spring and keep on a windowsill or in a glasshouse until they are ready to plant out once the weather starts to warm up.

CARE

Feed violas regularly if you grow them in pots. Hopefully you won't have too many flowers to deadhead because you'll be using the flowers to brighten up drinks and dishes, but don't leave faded blooms on the plant – snip them off to extend the flowering season. A light trim in midsummer will keep the plant looking compact and healthy. Come autumn, chop the plant back to about 5cm (2in) above the base.

PESTS & DISEASES

Slugs, snails and aphids.

HARVEST & STORAGE

Snip flowers off when young and pop them in cold water to keep them pert and plump. Use fresh, preferably the same day you pick them.

HOME REMEDIES

Traditionally, violas were used to make a syrup to treat sore throats. You can also use a tea made with violas as a gargle for sore throats and to help treat urinary tract infections. Combine fresh flowers with Epsom salts to make scented bath salts.

CULINARY USES

Crystallized violas can be used to decorate cakes. Making crystalized flowers is a simple process: paint each flower with egg white, dip the flower in caster sugar, place the flower on a sheet of baking parchment and let dry for about 24 hours. Once the crystallized flowers are completely dry, store them in an airtight container, separated by layers of baking parchment. Be warned: I didn't wait long enough for the flowers to dry with my first batch and I stored them on kitchen paper and they went soggy.

Violet syrup can be used to flavour drinks, cakes and desserts. To make a syrup, first, you'll need to infuse a handful of viola petals (without the calyx) in 1 cup boiling distilled water overnight. The next day, transfer the infused water to a heatproof glass bowl, add the same weight of caster sugar and set the bowl over a bain marie and heat until the sugar has dissolved. It's important to use distilled water and white sugar to make this syrup, otherwise you'll dilute the gorgeous blue colour.

Other ideas to try are ground petals combined with rice pudding and flavoured with almonds – a 14th century luxury – or to layer fresh flowers in a jar with caster sugar to make violet sugar. You can also use the infused water as a base flavour for jelly!

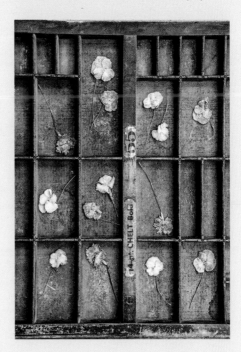

HERBS
&
SPICES

This was the hardest chapter to curate, as I found myself agonising about which plants to leave off rather than leave on the list… after all, when is a herb not a botanical (I wish I was witty enough to make that into a joke). In the end, I settled for a combination that looked good when planted together, like sweet cicely and angelica in my tetris borders, provided a flavour that to me reflected the current mood for botanically-flavoured drinks or would become a staple ingredient for everyday, easy-to-use remedies.

ALOE VERA

(ALOE VERA)

I'm a little embarrassed to admit that for some years now I've been having an ongoing battle with my parents about the benefits of using aloe vera versus arnica. My parents use aloe vera in a gel form to treat absolutely everything, which, with three grandchildren under thirteen, covers a lot of ground: burns, bumps, bruises and scratches all call for aloe vera in their home. Whereas, I think burns are best treated with aloe vera, while bumps and bruises are served better with arnica.

However, since researching this book, I now realize my parents have been right all along. I suppose the proof was always there – bruises never coloured up, scrapes didn't become infected and burns (thankfully, only ever minor ones) were soothed and disappeared quickly. In fact, the benefits of aloe vera aren't limited to these ailments.

Aloe vera is a must-have item for any natural medicine cabinet, and my son and I often have the telltale greenish-yellow stains on our skin where we've applied fresh aloe vera to prove it. Luckily, my plant has had babies, which means we won't be running out of aloe vera any time soon and there will be plants to share – if anyone deserves to have a plant of their own, it's my gorgeous folks.

GROW ☉ H 0.5-1M; W 0.5-1M

Native to Africa, this succulent can grow into a strikingly large, sculptural specimen if it's grown outside in hot, dry conditions. However, in cooler climates aloe vera is best grown as a houseplant. Plant it in an open sandy soil mix that drains well. It will need light but can cope with low light if you can't squeeze it onto your windowsill. While aloe vera needs regular watering, allow it to dry out between each drink. Overwatering will kill it, so find your groove by checking the soil regularly and keeping an eye out for signs of stress, like reddening and drooping of the leaves. Choosing a terracotta pot for the plant will also help as the container's material will dry out rather than retain moisture.

CARE

Aloe vera prefers its roots to fit cozily into a pot so you won't need to pot it up very often. However, if the plant becomes top-heavy, transfer it to a slightly bigger pot to stop it from toppling over. Remove baby plants that develop at the base and pot up, growing them on as a new specimens. You can also try taking leaf cuttings: cut a 7.5cm (3in) portion of stem and allow it to dry out for a week or so before gently pushing it into a pot of free-draining compost.

PESTS & DISEASES

Rot: leaf, soft, fungal and root.

HARVEST & STORAGE

Apply aloe vera directly to your skin by snapping off a leaf and letting the juice drip out. Alternatively, slit the entire leaf lengthways and scrape out the gel, which can be stored for up to 1 week in the refrigerator or frozen in ice-cube trays and then defrosted as required.

HOME REMEDIES

Aloe vera gel can be applied to minor burns (for anything more serious, consult a doctor), bruises, scratches, sunburn and cold sores. It's also a great hair conditioner if you mix it with equal parts water. Undiluted, aloe vera gel can be used as a natural styling gel.

CULINARY USES

Combine aloe vera gel with fruit juice or add it to a smoothie to give your skin and immune system a healthy boost and help with digestive disorders.

For poached aloe vera to serve with yogurt, peel 2 large aloe vera stems and cut the flesh into cubes. Place the aloe vera flesh in a saucepan with 2 tablespoons lime juice and 1 cup (180g/6 ¼ oz) sugar and cook over a medium heat until the aloe vera loses its slimy consistency. Leave to cool before adding to the yogurt.

HERBS & SPICES

LEMON VERBENA

(ALOYSIA CITRODORA)

When I asked my Instagram followers which botanical they wouldn't or couldn't live without, this pretty shrub was top of the list. I'm not surprised. It's easy to grow in containers (photographed here growing with Indian mint and bee balm) and borders and it looks absolutely beautiful in late summer, with elegant spires of pale flowers that tower above its narrow leaves. However, the real reason for its popularity is its incredible flavour, which is quite different to other lemon-scented herbs like lemon thyme, lemon mint and lemon balm. Lemon verbena testes like lemon sherbet. The plant even emits that sweet scent when you brush past it.

GROW ⬭ H 1.5-2.5M; W 1.5-2.5M

Lemon verbena comes originally from Argentina and Chile so it needs a sunny, sheltered spot, preferably against a south-facing wall. It benefits from a free-draining soil. If you don't have free-draining soil, add plenty of horticultural grit at planting time. Pinch out tips to help create a bushy plant and it will reach about 2.5m (8¼ft) in height and width after about 6 or 7 years.

CARE

Lemon verbena will be happy outside for most of the year, but you'll need to bring it indoors during very cold snaps because it can't cope with harsh frosts. If in doubt, err on the side of caution and bring the plant indoors over winter. In warmer climes, you can feel more confident about leaving it outside as long as you provide it with some winter protection.

Other than keeping an eye out for frost, lemon verbena is a low-maintenance perennial plant. Water regularly during the height of summer and feed with liquid seaweed every 2 weeks. It is deciduous and will drop its leaves in winter, so remember to gather them up and use them fresh or dry them. A quick chop in the autumn, reducing the plant to half its size, will ensure plenty of healthy growth the following season.

PESTS & DISEASES

Whitefly and spider mites.

HARVEST & STORAGE

Pick leaves from the base of the plant as they'll be older and tend to have a stronger flavour. The leaves can be used freshly picked for a vibrant, refreshing flavour or dried so you can have a year-round supply.

HOME REMEDIES

Use older leaves to make a tea that is great for sleeping problems, indigestion, heartburn and other digestive disorders.

CULINARY USES

Steep lemon verbena leaves in a sugar syrup to make an intensely zingy cordial that can be added to spritzers, cocktails and even ice creams and sorbets.

I've recently tried putting 2 cups fresh leaves and 90g (3¼oz) sugar in a food processor or blender and blitzing them to make a paste that can be frozen. To use, break off bits of the frozen mixture and add to dishes as a delicious sweet seasoning.

ANGELICA

(ANGELICA ARCHANGELICA)

I've always grown angelica because it has such presence, especially in a small plot. Like the tall bear-of-a friend who towers non-threateningly over everyone at a party, angelica is a rather elegant giant with huge arching leaves and, every other year, scented, larger-than-life, dome-shaped blooms.

Recently, I've read more about this plant and, more excitingly, tasted the incredibly delicious homemade candied stems. I really can't believe I've missed out on this rather satisfying preserving process for so many years. In fact, why isn't everyone candying angelica? As a rule, I've tended to ignore the call to use candied angelica and peel in my mother's Christmas cake recipe. However, this year I can't wait to make it with BOTH these ingredients … from my garden! Furthermore, candied angelica can be used as a straw. Eco-friendly, delicious and something Dorothy wouldn't have blinked an eye at had she seen them in the Emerald City – what's not to love about that idea?

Angelica belongs to the *Apiaceae* family, better known as the celery, carrot or parsley family, which explains its gorgeous umbelliferous flower heads. Bees and butterflies love angelica's flowers and birds will appreciate any seedheads left on the plant in autumn when they're on the hunt for food.

GROW ⬳ H 1.5-2.5M; W 1-1.5M

Angelica is a beinnial, which means a bit of patience is required before the plant reaches its full statuesque height and flowers in its second year. The plant often dies after flowering. Despite angelica's long/short lifecycle (depending on how you look at it), it's so worth growing the plant for what it adds to the garden, as well as the kitchen.

I usually buy them in small 9cm (3¾in) pots. Once established in the garden, the plant will self-seed, so you should be set for a constant supply of angelica. If you don't want the plant to self-seed, simply deadhead after flowering.

If you're starting off by seed, sow in spring and leave on a windowsill or in the glasshouse. The seeds need light to germinate, so only cover them with a thin layer of soil. Pot on seedlings into 9cm (3¾in) pots. When the roots start to poke out of the bottom of the pots, plant out in a border or good-sized containers as it will reach 1.5m (5ft) in height.

It grows in Scandinavia, Greenland, Iceland, central Europe and some parts of northern Asia. The plant will do well in full sun or partial shade but it will only grow in damp soil. It can cope with clay soil but prefers moist, well-draining soil if possible.

CARE

The plant might need staking. When growing from seed, plant out the seedlings when young as older plants resent disturbance.

PESTS & DISEASES

Aphids, snails, slugs and, if the summer is very dry, powdery mildew.

CONTINUED...

HARVEST & STORAGE

Cut stems in the second year when they are young and tender, ready to candy. Lift tender roots in the autumn and store in an airtight container.

HOME REMEDIES

Angelica was well known among the Vikings. According to the Icelandic Sagas, the plant was protected by law from overharvesting until the year 1000. In Norway, the plant was cultivated in special gardens and it was probably the first medicinal plant that was exported to the rest of Europe, hence its common name, Norwegian angelica. This bitter herb is primarily used for ailments associated with the digestive system. A tea made from angelica is purported to improve lost appetites. Add 1 teaspoon dried and finely chopped angelica root to 1 cup boiling water and let it steep for a few minutes before straining and drinking the tea. The crushed leaves are said to reduce travel sickness. Additionally, if the leaves are stewed and added to bathwater, angelica is said to relieve rheumatism and aching muscles.

CULINARY USES

The stems are rich in nutrients and can be eaten in the same way as celery. The outer layer of the stems is usually removed and the green and juicy inner parts are eaten. For candied angelica, preserve young hollow stems in sugar. Angelica has been used as a flavouring agent in liqueurs for centuries and it is still the main flavour in the French liqueurs Bénédictine and Chartreuse. The roots and stems smell strongly of gin, so it's no surprise that this is one of the botanicals used in the flavouring of gins and vermouths. You can use angelica seeds in pastries and to flavour jams, preserves, chutneys, bitters, liqueurs and gins.

CHERVIL

(ANTHRISCUS CEREFOLIUM)

I grew chervil for the first time this year. This herb is easy to grow, pretty, has a delicate aniseed flavour and isn't widely available in supermarkets, which begs the question: why hadn't I tried it before?

The wild form of chervil is cow parsley, the much-loved lacy summer umbellifer. However, wild chervil's flavour isn't as strong as cultivated chervil and there's also the problem that it looks for all the world like hemlock, which is poisonous. So homegrown chervil is definitely the better option here.

GROW ⬭ H 0.1–0.5M; W 0.1–0.5M

Sow seed in the ground between spring and late summer or sow the seed in small pots and grow until the plants are established enough to move into larger containers. This perennial herb prefers the shade and will run to seed if it's left in the sunshine.

CARE

Water regularly. Remove flowers to encourage plenty of leaf growth and stop the plant from self-seeding. Chervil is a useful winter crop if you can protect it with a cloche.

PESTS & DISEASES

Aphids, slugs and snails.

HARVEST & STORAGE

Pick young fresh growth before the plant has a chance to flower. Chervil is really best used fresh as freezing or drying weakens the herb's already subtle flavour.

HOME REMEDIES

Chervil is a Lenten herb: it was made into a soup and eaten on Maundy Thursday because it was thought to have blood-cleansing and restorative properties.

Chervil tea helps with circulatory disorders, liver complaints and chronic catarrh. The fresh leaves can be made into a warm poultice to apply to aching joints.

CULINARY USES

Chervil has a subtle flavour that's lost in cooking so it's best to add it to a dish just before serving. The fresh leaves can be used to flavour white wine and vinegar. In French cuisine, chervil is one of a classic combination of herbs called "Fines Herbes", the others being chives, tarragon and parsley.

FRENCH TARRAGON

(ARTEMISIA DRACUNCULUS)

During my early teens, I used to cook chicken in tarragon as my "fancy dish" for special family occasions. Don't judge me, it was the eighties. I remember the aniseed flavour was aromatic, light and totally moerish. While I might not cook that dish anymore (although writing this book has inspired me to try it again), I have a soft spot for this herb.

Go for French rather than Russian tarragon – I'm not commenting on those two nations here, just the former has a much stronger flavour than the latter.

GROW ⬭ H 0.5-1M; W 0.01-0.5M

You can't raise French tarragon from seed so you'll need to buy young plants. Tarragon won't survive winter frosts so it'll really appreciate it if you find it a spot on your windowsill. If you want to grow it in the garden, find a sunny spot but keep it in a container and protect during the cold months. Make sure the compost is gritty and free-draining.

CARE

Keep the plant well-watered, but don't let it become waterlogged. Pinch out flowers to encourage plenty of new growth and prevent it getting too tall and spindly. Take cuttings in early summer – the plants tend to get a bit tired and worn out after a few years.

PESTS & DISEASES

Powdery mildew and rust.

HARVEST & STORAGE

Pick stems and strip the leaves with your fingers. Use fresh leaves during the summer months; they will keep in a plastic bag in the refrigerator. The dried leaves lose their flavour quickly, so keep them in an airtight container.

HOME REMEDIES

Tarragon contains eugenol, the same pain-relieving essential oil found in clove oil, so chew fresh leaves or drink tarragon tea if you have sore gums or toothache. Tarragon tea is a popular remedy in France for treating insomnia and it's thought to be a good appetite stimulant. Putting a tarragon sprig in each shoe before a long walk is said to give you strength. (I'm not sure about that, perhaps strength is gained by ignoring the discomfort of having a sprig in your shoe!) You can dilute tarragon oil and use it as a natural deodorant.

CULINARY USES

Tarragon is considered by the French to be one of the "Fab Four" seasoning ingredients (though I don't think that's the official slogan). Fresh tarragon can be used to flavour vinegar and oil or be made into a syrup to add to cocktails and soft drinks.

CAROLINA ALLSPICE

(CALYCANTHUS FLORIDUS)

I'm excited to be growing this hardy shrub because it's quite rare in the UK, though it shouldn't be because it's fairly easy to grow. In the USA it thrives in the Appalachian and Smoky Mountain regions. I love the idea of walking by great thickets of this shrub, as the air must be filled with its gorgeous spicy fragrance.

Despite its name, you can't consume all of this plant: the flowers and seeds aren't edible. Its bark, however, can be dried, crushed and used as a substitute for cinnamon, which is really thrilling because cinnamon is considerably harder to grow as it really benefits from a tropical climate.

GROW ✧ H 2.5-3.5M; W 3.5-4M

Choose a sunny spot for Carolina allspice and provide it with moist, well-drained soil with plenty of organic matter, though I've read it'll cope with most soil types and isn't fussed about a bit of shade. It's a tough customer and doesn't mind being buffeted about in the wind, which is a useful quality when many plants featured in this book do prefer a bit of shelter.

CARE

Feed and water it regularly during the growing season. Once the plant is established and produces buds in spring, cut back the stems to about 4 buds from the base and apply a mulch of well-rotted manure around the base. During the growing season, make sure the centre of the bush isn't too congested. If it is, thin a few stems to ensure good circulation around the plant.

PESTS & DISEASES

Powdery mildew.

HARVEST & STORAGE

Snip off twigs to dry and use as a substitute for cinnamon.

HOME REMEDIES

The leaves contain small amounts of camphor so can be used as an insect repellent.

CULINARY USES

Only use the bark of this plant in the kitchen, never the flowers or seeds. You can use the bark to make a tea or flavour wine.

TEA CAMELLIA

(CAMELLIA SINENSIS VAR. SINENSIS)

The tea camellia isn't rare. In fact, it is so widely used in tea production that it is ubiquitous. However, I love the idea of its history and the great social changes associated with tea. Growing it and being able to make my own tea from its glossy green leaves feels poignant. The plant hunter Robert Fortune introduced the tea camellia to the Indian Himalayas from China on behalf of the British East India Company, and the rest is, well, history. While the tea plantation plants aren't allowed to form flowers, it does have a small, pretty flower in autumn. That said, it's all about the leaves…

GROW ✋ H 2.5-3M; W 1.5-2M

If you live in a mild location, have a sheltered spot and some space, you can grow this camellia outdoors. (Did you know there are UK tea plantations in Cornwall and Scotland?) I keep my plant in the glasshouse and move it into the kitchen during the winter, which brightens up a corner of the room rather nicely. It needs acid soil, so if your soil is alkaline or neutral, growing it in a container with ericaceous compost is probably your best bet.

CARE

This plant's top three dislikes are the cold, dry winds and early morning sun. Otherwise, it's pretty unfussy. It prefers not to be left to dry out in summer, so water regularly and feed in mid-spring and midsummer. Add a handful of leaf mould on top of the soil in spring. If you're growing in a container, wrap with hessian, newspaper or bubble wrap in winter to keep frosts at bay. Don't worry if the leaves brown a little at the edges, from conditions being too humid, as it won't affect new growth.

PESTS & DISEASES

Aphids, scale insects, vine weevils and leaf spot.

HARVEST & STORAGE

The best – and most flavoursome – leaves are the new growth, which appear and can be picked in spring. Wait a year or two before picking the leaves to allow the plant to establish itself. The flavour of the leaves will vary according to the soil and climate in which the plant is grown, the way the leaves are harvested and the manner in which they're processed after picking. The leaves can be used fresh or dried. Dried leaves should be stored in an airtight container.

HOME REMEDIES

Tea offers a bewildering array of health benefits, from helping to stop tooth cavities due to its natural fluorine levels to aiding weight loss and reducing the risk of cancer. I have started to use tea-infused water as a mouthwash. Steep 5–8 dried leaves in a cup, depending on how strong you like your tea.

CULINARY USES

Green tea is made by steaming freshly picked leaves for just under a minute or roasting the leaves in a hot pan for a couple of minutes. This procedure is called sha-quing ("killing out" in Chinese), which refers to the oxidizing enzymes that are destroyed during this process. If you let the tea leaves oxidize and dry naturally for half an hour, then let them dry for a further 4– 5 hours, crush and bruise them by rolling them in your hands and finally put them in a preheated oven at 90°C (200°F) for 5 minutes to dry out, you'll make oolong tea. For black tea, it's the same process as for oolong, but the leaves are allowed to oxidize for longer after they have been crushed – they are left on a tray in a shady location for up to 3 days – before being dried out in the oven for 5 minutes.

CARAWAY

(CARUM CARVI)

This is a very pretty plant to have in your garden but you'll need to be patient; it's a biennial so it won't produce flowers until the second summer. However, once it has flowered you'll be rewarded with a harvest of delectable liquorice-flavoured seeds. I chose individual containers for my caraway plants, to combine with the salad burnet (see page 94) on my windowsill, but caraway will look equally good partnered with any plants with contrasting textures and leaf shapes, such as anise hyssop (see page 52), bergamot (see page 84) and nigella (see page 143).

GROW ✏ H 0.6M; W 0.2M

Caraway likes full sun or partial shade and, ideally, sandy soil. It has long taproots, which are edible and can be treated just like you would parsnips.

CARE

Cut back at the end of the first season to help encourage fresh new growth in the second year. Caraway will self-seed happily if you leave some seeds on the plant.

PESTS & DISEASES

No real issues.

HARVEST & STORAGE

Caraway leaves can be picked throughout the growing season and used fresh or dried.

Harvest the seeds in the second year once they turn a rich deep-brown colour. To collect the seeds, cut the umbels off the plant, put them in a paper bag and let them dry in the open bag for a few days before shaking the bag to detach the seeds.

HOME REMEDIES

Chew caraway seeds to help indigestion and flatulence – there's a reference to the seed being used by the over-indulging Falstaff in Shakespeare's *Henry IV*. You can also infuse the seeds in water to make a mouthwash to freshen breath.

CULINARY USES

The young and tender leaves are best and can be used in salads. The dried leaves can be used year round as you would any other dried herb. The seeds can be used to make a tea or flavoured alcohol.

HERBS & SPICES

SAFFRON CROCUS

(CROCUS SATIVUS)

Growing my own saffron was an item on my bucket list for many years; each time I thought about doing it, it would be autumn and too late to buy the corms and plant them. Saffron eluded me in my role as a garden editor, too. On several occasions I attempted to commission features about savvy saffron growers who were endeavouring to produce it on a more commercial scale, only for them to have a change of heart about appearing in the magazine. So perhaps you can imagine how incredibly satisfying it felt to finally plant 50 corms in my garden on a warm afternoon as the summer was drawing to an end. From that crop I harvested a little over 0.25g of dried saffron (you need about 150 flowers to make one gram), and seeing those gorgeous bright-orange strands felt pretty darn good.

GROW ☙ H 0.1M; W 0.1M

The saffron crocus is easy to grow if you provide it with very well-drained compost. Choose a sunny spot and plant 10–15cm (4–6in) deep and about 10cm (4in) apart. The corms will bulk up over the years.

CARE

This plant doesn't need to be watered, but if it's particularly dry during early autumn, water it once. After a couple of frosts, dig up the corms, place them in a wooden box or tray and cover them with sand. Store somewhere cool and dry and then plant out again in spring. After about 5 years, divide congested areas right after the flowers have faded, either planting them in smaller groups elsewhere in the garden or gifting to friends.

PESTS & DISEASES

Mice and voles like to nibble the corms.

HARVEST & STORAGE

Saffron is the most expensive spice in the world because it's so fiddly and time-consuming to harvest. Expect flowers about 6 weeks after planting. Don't worry if not all the bulbs bloom in the first year, by the second year most bulbs will give about two flowers each. The saffron strands are actually the stigma of the flower, and each flower produces three. Carefully remove the stigmas with tweezers and lay them out on kitchen paper to dry thoroughly over the course of a few days. Once dried, store the saffron in an airtight jar.

HOME REMEDIES

Saffron tea is said to be a mood enhancer. You can use saffron-infused milk as a toner to brighten dull skin or saffron-infused rosewater to help your skin look younger.

CULINARY USES

Use saffron sparingly to add a delicate colour and flavour to dishes, including curries, risottos, paellas, bread and other baked items, jams and sauces.

TURMERIC

(CURCUMA LONGA)

You won't be surprised to discover that turmeric isn't going to do well in a cool climate without a bit of pampering. Coming from South and Southeast Asia, it will sulk if it isn't basking in balmy temperatures. Don't be put off though – that's easy to sort with a bottom-heat mat, heated propagator or a bright position indoors. Once you've got its location sorted out, the rest is fairly straightforward, given the rich rewards.

GROW ✥ H 1.5-2M; W0.5-1M

Start by getting your tubers in early spring. If you're lucky, you'll be able to find them in your local greengrocer or supermarket – you're looking for nice plump sections. Or find suppliers online. Encourage them to sprout (or "chit") by putting them in a cool, light place where they won't be zapped by the frost – a windowsill is often fine. Once they've got shoots, plant in a 45cm (1½ft) pot, with the roots facing downward and the shoots (or "eyes") facing upward and just peeping out of the soil – to help prevent them rotting. They will need gentle but constant heat, so either place the pot in a propagator or cover it with a clear plastic bag to provide some humidity. You'll need to pot on the plants as they grow and find a warm, dry, frost-free spot for them to overwinter.

CARE

You'll need to monitor the temperature to make sure it's around 21°C (70°F). Feed regularly as it is a hungry devil, and keep an eye on the soil to make sure it doesn't dry out too quickly.

PESTS & DISEASES

Leaf spot, though I think this is mostly an issue in commercially grown crops.

HARVEST & STORAGE

It's better to wait until the plants' second year before you harvest to alow the rhizomes to bulk up and make stronger plants. Wait until the leaves start dying back in late autumn to early winter before you harvest. When harvested, the rhizome should be bigger than it was when you first planted it. Ideally, you want enough to be able to use some of the rhizome to store and replant ready for next year and keep the remaining section for cooking and home remedies. Wrap the rhizome in kitchen paper and store it in an airtight container in the refrigerator (it will keep for a couple of weeks) or freeze it in chunks in freezer-safe bags. If you want to replant it next year, dig up the rhizomes at the end of the growing season when the leaves turn yellow. Wash off the dirt and store somewhere dry, dark and cool until late winter or early spring when new sprouts appear on the rhizomes. Cut the rhizomes into sections, making sure that each segment has a sprout, bud or eye and replant.

HOME REMEDIES

In recent years, turmeric has made the headlines for its natural anti-inflammatory, antioxidant and detoxification properties because it contains the compound curcumin. Turmeric tea is a good way to reap the benefits: put a few slices of fresh turmeric and fresh ginger in a saucepan with 300ml (10fl oz) water and a twist of black pepper and simmer for 30 minutes, remove from the heat and leave it to steep overnight. If you add coconut milk and honey to turmeric tea, you'll transform it into golden milk.

CULINARY USES

Use grated turmeric to flavour smoothies, juices and scrambled eggs. Thin slices can be pickled by placing them in a mixture of lemon juice, salt and chilli and letting the mixture ferment for 3 days.

HERBS & SPICES

LEMONGRASS

(CYMBOPOGON CITRATUS)

I've cooked with lemongrass for many years, but until this year I'd never grown it myself. As I harvested my first stem, I wondered why it had taken me so long to try growing it in my garden. I suppose I'd always assumed lemongrass was an exotic plant that wouldn't fare well in the UK's climate. However, it's actually pretty robust and is happy to languish outdoors in the sunshine all summer long. Given the current fashion for grasses, it's also an excellent plant for a small garden, providing soft fountains of lush green spikes that rustle and sway in the wind.

GROW ✧ H 1-1.5M; W 0.5-1M

You can buy plug plants (as I did) or grow lemongrass from seed, sowing it in small pots in spring and using a heated propagator to get them going – well, they are used to tropical temperatures. Pot them on as they grow, but make sure the plants are quite established before putting them outside – the Royal Horticultural Society recommends waiting until they're big enough for a 20cm (8in) pot. You can even grow this perennial plant from shop-bought stems, popping them in pots until roots appear and then potting them up. Choose a sunny spot for them and keep them well watered.

CARE

At the end of the summer, bring lemongrass indoors so you can keep it in the manner to which it is accustomed, with temperatures no lower than 5°C (41°F). The foliage will turn brown in autumn, at which point cut back to about 10cm (4in). When you see new growth in spring, start feeding and watering regularly.

PESTS & DISEASES

None to worry about, apart from the odd snail.

HARVEST & STORAGE

Harvest stems as and when needed. If a clump is quite tightly packed, use a knife to remove a section and then prise the stems free. A good tip is to take a section off the stem and plant it, using the remainder in the kitchen – that way you're not completely depleting stocks. Fresh is best when it comes to lemongrass, though cut stems can be stored in the refrigerator for a few weeks or they can be frozen. To dry lemongrass, tie it in bundles and hang upside down.

HOME REMEDIES

Lemongrass is a bit of a marvellous medicine. Drunk as a tea, lemongrass can aid digestion, reduce anxiety, act as a diuretic and detox your system, as well as relieve pain, reduce blood pressure, boost your immune system and fight flu and cold symptoms. Oh, and chewing on the stems freshens breath.

Lemongrass can also be used as a mosquito repellent: simply crush the leaves to release their oil and rub it on your skin.

CULINARY USES

If you want to use lemongrass in your cooking, you should only use the bottom 7cm (2½in) of the stem, chopping or pounding it to a pulp in a pestle and mortar. (The discarded top sections of the stems can be strewn along borders or around containers to deter insects.) Entire lemongrass stems can be used to flavour vodka.

CARDAMOM

(ELETTARIA CARDAMOMUM)

Cardamom is part of the ginger family, which you can see in its leaf growth and the flower (when it eventually appears). It's not only the seeds of green cardamom that are scented – each time I brush past the plant in the glasshouse it releases a spicy and warm fragrance that's truly intoxicating.

I'm really thrilled about how well the cardamom in my glasshouse has grown this year. I bought a small plant in a 10cm (4in) pot on eBay and coaxed it into growing for the first month in my kitchen, where it settled in quite happily until I felt it had outgrown the kitchen shelf and required something more in the way of care and attention. Cardamom is said to be the third most expensive spice, after saffron and vanilla. I'm dying to harvest my plant, but I'll need to be patient and wait another two years to let it mature and flower.

GROW ✎ H 2-4M; W 1-2M

In its native southern India, cardamom blooms all year round and grows up to 6m (20ft) tall. However, in cooler and drier climates it needs plenty of attention and coaxing to do well, and even then, reaching that height might be ambitious. From mid-spring onwards, I transfer my plant to the glasshouse and endeavour to mist it every day in an effort to recreate the humid temperatures of the rainforests it loves. As soon as the weather turns in autumn, I'll bring it back indoors as it won't be happy if the temperature drops much below 22°C (72°F). You can grow cardamom indoors all year round, but it will need to have a really good spot that will allow it to spread out as it matures. It also needs plenty of indirect light (between 6–8 hours) and humidity, so a bright, hot, steamy bathroom could be ideal. You can give cardamom a further helping hand by providing slightly acidic compost. Use a 50:50 compost/ericaceous mix and top-dress with more ericaceous compost each year to try to maintain that pH balance.

CARE

It needs humidity and mustn't be allowed to dry out, though it also won't cope if it's waterlogged. Feed weekly with a foliage plant food during the growing season. Once it's matured and reached a good size, split the rhizomes to make new plants.

PESTS & DISEASES

Cardamom mosaic virus and rhizome rot.

HARVEST & STORAGE

Once the plant flowers, allow the seed capsules to dry and develop on the plant. When they turn green, pick off and continue to dry on screens, turning daily.

HOME REMEDIES

A tea made from the leaves can be used as a gargle to relieve sore throats and ease indigestion. Boil roasted seeds and add them to tea to make a tonic to relieve the symptoms of stress. Nibble cardamom seeds to freshen breath and aid digestion.

CULINARY USES

For a cardamom-infused water to serve as a refreshing soft drink, boil the seeds in water, then strain and allow to cool. You can also use the seeds to flavour mulled wine, mocktails, spirits, lemonade, custards, rice and curries.

HERBS & SPICES

FENNEL

(FOENICULUM VULGARE)

I'm a foodie. I devour recipe books, cook food from scratch, eat out as much as my wallet allows and even started an alternative to a book club for my friends, where we each bring a cooked dish to our gatherings and talk about cookery and cookbooks. However, I've always drawn the line at what I consider to be pretentious food: when a chef seems to be trying too hard, sacrificing flavour and honest ingredients for fancy tricks and gimmicks.

Over the years, I revelled in the moral high ground, that was until I discovered fennel pollen (#shetypesblushingatthehypocrisy). One day, I interviewed a chef and he talked about harvesting fennel pollen because it's

sweeter and has a far more intense flavour than fennel seeds. (I should point out, because it can get confusing, that he was referring to the perennial herb, not the bulb-forming variety of fennel, known as Florence fennel.) Now, I love fennel seeds, so the idea of something that tasted even more aniseedy was intriguing. My interest was piqued, even though I thought it all sounded a bit chichi, so back at home, and in secret, I picked a few fennel flowers and dutifully shook them onto some paper. The chef was right: before I'd even tasted the pollen, the smell was sensational; and the flavour was surprisingly sweet, with notes of citrus and liquorice.

Fennel pollen enhances the flavour of whatever it's added to, which is pretty awesome, and it's such a gorgeous colour, too. You can buy it online, but it's super expensive. Do you need any other reasons to give it a try?

GROW ⬙ H 1.5-2.5M; W 0.5-1M

Plant fennel in full sunshine with moist, well-drained soil or grow it in container. It's a great plant if you want a bit of height and interest but don't want to wait a few years. Direct sow in mid-spring when the soil has warmed and it'll be about 2m (6½ft) tall by the summer. Bronze fennel (*Foeniculum vulgare* 'Purpureum') is hardier than common fennel.

CARE

Don't move the plant once it's sown, it doesn't like its roots being disturbed. No ongoing maintenance is required, apart from removing fading flowers to prevent self-seeding.

PESTS & DISEASES

Aphids can take up residence.

HARVEST & STORAGE

Pick seeds when they're green for a juicy experience or let them dry on the flower before harvesting. As I've already mentioned, you can collect pollen by shaking fresh flowers onto a white plate or into a paper bag. I prefer the former technique because it allows the collection of tiny bugs that may also fall from the blooms to escape. The more gently you shake the flowers, the less flotsam and jetsam appears. You can snip off the fresh tips of feathery foliage, which tastes of aniseed.

HOME REMEDIES

Fennel seeds can be chewed to freshen your breath. The seeds can also be used to make a calming tea that can soothe the symptoms of food poisoning, be used as a gargle for sore throats and be drunk prior to eating or chewed after eating as a remedy for flatulence. To make the tea, bruise the seeds and then steep them in boiling water for 10 minutes.

CULINARY USES

The seeds can be used to make a tea and the leaves can be infused in oil or vinegar. You can prepare a delicious digestive chew by combining fennel seeds, anise seeds, cardamom seeds, orange peel and chopped, crystallized ginger. I've also seen an interesting idea online, which calls for dried lavender, bay leaves, fennel seeds, cumin seeds, rose petals, nutmeg, cloves and peppercorns to be roasted and then ground and steeped in oil to make a version of the popular spice mix ras el hanout. Fennel seeds are used in Mediterranean and Middle Eastern dishes as well.

Fennel pollen can be used as a seasoning for savoury and sweet dishes, but use it sparingly – a smidgen goes a long way. The pollen adds a killer final flourish to a Bloody Mary cocktail.

LIQUORICE

(GLYCYRRHIZA GLABRA)

Discovering I could grow my own liquorice root here in the UK is a great example of why it's been so enjoyable to research and grow plants for this book. I love liquorice; I remember my grandparents buying wheels of black liquorice with the colourful liquorice-flavoured bobbly sweet in the middle. While I don't expect to be able to make my own liquorice, having the flavour to play with is an exciting prospect.

Like turmeric (see page 122), liquorice is a perennial plant that requires you to be patient while you wait for the root to become sufficiently mature to harvest. To give you a sense of what the plant will look like after a few years in your garden, Tory photographed a well-established specimen at the University of Bristol Botanic Garden (see opposite).

GROW ⟴ H 1M; W 1M

To grow liquorice, choose a good-sized container for a young plant or find space at the back of a border because once this plant gets going it will reach about 2m (6½ft) in height, with a spread of about 1m (3¼ft). Liquorice prefers a sunny spot with moist, almost boggy, soil (it grows on riverbanks in the wild), but it'll cope with most soil types. Keep it sheltered so its delicate foliage doesn't get damaged. You can grow it from seed if you're not in a great rush to be able to harvest it.

CARE

Water well but don't worry too much about feeding. Cut back in autumn, ready for new growth to appear the following spring.

PESTS & DISEASES

Generally free from pests and diseases.

HARVEST & STORAGE

You'll have to wait at least a couple of years before you can harvest the root. Once the plant is mature, harvest annually to prevent the roots from becoming too big or competing with other plants if it's grown in the ground. Alternate the side from which you harvest each autumn. Don't cut the main taproots, instead choose the side roots that appear closer to the surface of the soil and are a bright yellow-brown colour.

HOME REMEDIES

The name for liquorice is derived from the Greek *glycyrrhiza*, which means "sweet root". Chew freshly harvested roots to enjoy the sticky-sweet sap, which can help treat constipation, ulcers and various stomach disorders.

To make lozenges to soothe a sore throat, put 2.5cm- (1in-) long sections of liquorice root in a saucepan, add just enough water to cover the roots and boil until they are soft. When soft (test with a knife), strain, return the pieces of root to the pan and mash to make a paste. Transfer teaspoonfuls of the mixture to baking parchment and let dry. Store in an airtight jar for up to 6 months in dry conditions.

CULINARY USES

You can steep liquorice root in boiling water to make a nourishing tea or plunge it into a jar of sugar to create a flavoured sugar for making cakes.

HERBS & SPICES

BAY

(LAURUS NOBILIS)

I love bay leaves and use them in lots of my recipes, from a pear and bay cake to the perfect basmati rice. The shrub itself totally appeals to me because it's evergreen and behaves well if it's pruned into a neat ball shape or topiarized to make a standard tree.

I bought a ball-shaped bay for my garden earlier this year and found, as with so many of my online purchases, that I had ordered an enormous specimen. When it was delivered, everyone looked at the shrub and then at the front door, trying to decide whether it would actually fit through the doorway. Thankfully, it did, and I think the garden is all the better for the huge-domed bay that screens the seating area from the kitchen window. This large bay guarantees me a lifetime supply of bay leaves, providing I take care of it, of course, and it supports the notion that you don't have to think small if you have a tiny garden.

GROW ⊝ H 8-12M; W 8+M

Bay trees are just as happy to be grown in a decent-sized container as they are in the ground, which is great news if you only have a balcony or a courtyard garden. Choose a sheltered spot and make sure your bay has at least a few hours of sun each day.

CARE

Water regularly when required, but don't overwater as the roots won't thank you if they're in soggy soil. If your bay is grown in the ground, protect the foliage with bubble wrap or horticultural fleece at first risk of frost. For container-grown plants, wrap the container in bubble wrap over winter. Prune regularly to encourage new growth and remove any damaged leaf tips in late spring. Take softwood or semi-ripe cuttings in summer or grow more plants from seed collected in the autumn.

PESTS & DISEASES

Leaf spot, yellow leaves and bay sucker.

HARVEST & STORAGE

Snip off leaves as and when required. To dry leaves, lay them on a rack to dry, then store in airtight jars.

HOME REMEDIES

Put 2 or 3 bay leaves in 1 cup (250ml/9floz) boiling water and let infuse for 10 minutes. Soak a cloth in the infused water and apply to your chest to help relieve colds, coughs and flu symptoms.

A tea made from bay leaves can help break a fever. I've also read, but haven't tested, that the tea can treat dandruff and hair loss.

To make bay leaf powder, crush or grind dried leaves into a powder. Used every few days, this can help to brighten teeth. A paste made with bay leaf powder and oil can soothe bites and stings.

CULINARY USES

There are all manner of culinary uses for bay leaves. Oil and vinegar infused with bay leaves are a great way to introduce interesting flavours to home-cooked dishes.

LOVAGE

(LEVISTICUM OFFICINALE)

In terms of looks, lovage is a little like celery and flat-leaved parsley on steroids, which is a good thing, just in case you were in any doubt. Its flavour is stronger than celery and has a hint of aniseed.

Lovage provides lush foliage all summer long and reaches up to 2m (6½ft) in height, which means it's a lovely specimen to grow in a container and it's a bit of a star in the border. This herb is actually a member of the carrot family, so produces those gorgeous umbel-shaped flowers during midsummer.

GROW ⬭ H 1.5-2.5M; W 0.5-1M

Lovage is easy to get started from seed if you have the space and time to get going in early spring, ready to plant out between mid-spring and early summer. It likes rich soil that is kept moist and will be just as happy in sun as it is in partial shade.

Try building up earth around the base of the stems (also known as earthing up) or wrap them in paper to block out light and blanch the stems, transforming them into tender veggies.

CARE

Trim in the summer to ensure a supply of fresh new growth. As the plant starts to fade in autumn, cut it back to ground level and, if you can, cover with a cloche – it'll appreciate a bit of protection from the cold wet weather. After a few years, you can lift and divide the plant in spring.

PESTS & DISEASES

Leaf miner.

HARVEST & STORAGE

Try to pick leaves before the flowers appear.

HOME REMEDIES

Drink a tea made from the leaves to help digestion or calm an upset stomach. Grated root infused in water can be used as a gargle to soothe sore throats.

CULINARY USES

In addition to using the leaves in soups, sauces, stews and salads, the stalks can be candied like angelica (see page 109), the dried leaves made into a tea and the seeds used to flavour dishes. I've even read that crushing a few leaves and adding them to whisky is delicious.

I recently discovered lovage cordial online. Originally created by Bristol's oldest wine merchant, Phillips of Bristol, lovage cordial is one of a range of herb-based cordials (actually liqueurs) that were made in the 1800s to treat and prevent illness on long sea voyages.

LEMON BALM

(MELISSA OFFICINALIS)

Lemon balm is an underrated herb that has lots of uses both in the kitchen and bathroom, making it a must-have perennial plant to try in your plot. Also known as bee balm, as you might guess, this plant is loved by bees. In fact, the Greek word for "bee" is *melissa*. The leaves lose their lemony potency after flowering so allow some stems to flower but remove others to keep a balance of fresh growth and happy wildlife.

GROW ⬙ H 0.5-1M; W 0.1-0.5M

A member of the mint family, this plant will grow happily in most soils and likes sun, though it will put up with a bit of shade. Lemon balm self-seeds prolifically and can take over so it's probably best to contain it in a good-sized pot and remove flowers before they set seed.

CARE

Plants need to be kept well-watered. Cut back after flowering to help encourage a second flush of leaves. Lift and divide large plants in late spring.

PESTS & DISEASES

Powdery mildew.

HARVEST & STORAGE

Pick leaves as and when required. If you're drying leaves, pick them before the flowers appear.

HOME REMEDIES

Crushed leaves keep mosquitoes at bay and can relieve the itch when applied to an insect bite. Chew a fresh leaf to freshen your breath. For a hair rinse for oily hair, combine fresh leaves with apple cider vinegar and let steep for a few weeks before using.

For a quick-and-easy bath soak, hang a muslin bag filled with lemon balm leaves (along with a few mint leaves, see page 138, and rose petals, see page 88, if you've got those in your garden too) on the tap in your bathtub and let the water run through it.

To make an infused oil, infuse crushed dried leaves in olive or sunflower oil for a month. The oil can be used to make salves, soaps and even a balm that can help cure cold sores.

Lemon balm tea is said to help restore memory and relieve the symptoms of stress. Made into a concentrated tea, lemon balm can aid sleep, even for children. To make such a tea, put some fresh leaves in a saucepan with enough water to cover them and simmer until the liquid is reduced by half. Strain and mix in a few teaspoons of honey to taste while the tea is still warm. Refrigerate for about 3 days and then take a spoonful of the tea before bed each night.

CULINARY USES

You can candy the leaves as you would rose petals and viola flowers (see page 100) or add the leaves to a glass of water for a citrus flavour.

MINT

(MENTHA SPP.)

Mint is a must for the botanical gardener. It's easy to grow, copes in most conditions and will reward minimal efforts with a long season of leaves that can be used in myriad different ways. I've grown mint in containers for years, tending to stick to the common apple mint and spearmint. However, I think I've been missing a trick because there are so many different flavours of mint available, each with its own distinctive quality, be it the texture of its leaves, its habit or its colour, including some very pretty variegated types.

I urge you to be experimental and pop some of the more unusual types of mint on your kitchen windowsill or near the kitchen door so they're quick and easy to pick. Here's a selection of interesting mints to try:

- Chocolate mint (*Mentha × piperita* f. *citrata* 'Chocolate') can be added to chocolate-flavoured puddings.

- Grapefruit mint (*Mentha × piperita* f. *citrata* 'Grapefruit') has a deliciously sharp citrus flavour.

- Lime mint (*Mentha × piperita* f. *citrata* 'Lime') has a refreshing lime scent and flavour.

- Black peppermint (*Mentha × piperita* black peppermint) is delicious when combined with black tea.

- Ginger mint (*Mentha x gracilis*) has pretty striped leaves with a distinctive scent and flavour.

- Sweet pear mint (*Mentha* 'Jessica's Sweet Pear') has a sweet flavour and a pear-like scent.

- Indian mint (*Satureja douglasii* 'Indian Mint') is a trailing variety with very dainty white flowers that looks quite different to traditional mints. Its delicate flavour is suited to tea.

- Spanish mint (*Mentha spicata*) has a strong spearmint flavour.

GROW ◐ H 0.5-1M; W 1-1.5MM

Mint tends to take over whenever it's given the opportunity, so it's a good idea to plant it in pots to restrict its roots, then plunge those pots in the border or in a larger container. Mint likes moist soil and a sunny spot, though it's more than happy in shade too. To make the most of my space, I've grown some of my herbs together, keeping them in individual pots within a larger container. Herbs can lose their individual flavour when grown together like this, but I haven't found that to be the case with my herbs.

CARE

Cut this perennial back to the ground once it has finished flowering. When the plant becomes pot-bound, lift out and divide to make two or three new plants. If you don't have room for more mint, gift new plants to your friends.

PESTS & DISEASES

Rust and mint beetle.

HARVEST & STORAGE

As with so many herbs, snipping off leaves and tips regularly keeps the plant looking its best. The young leaves have more flavour, so start harvesting as soon as the plant comes up in spring, though don't go too mad. Fresh mint sprigs keep for a few days in water and leaves can be frozen or air-dried in bunches.

HOME REMEDIES

Mint is a calming herb that has been used for thousands of years to aid upset stomachs and indigestion. It's also great for freshening breath: chew on some leaves, drink mint tea or try making homemade toothpaste. To relieve a tension headache, apply a compress of mint leaves to your forehead.

CULINARY USES

You can make delicious teas, flavour vinegars and oils and create soups and sauces. and, of course, you can't beat a mint julep or mojito made with homegrown mint.

SWEET CICELY

(MYRRHIS ODORATA)

While I like the idea of sweet cicely's fern-like leaves providing some contrasting texture in my Tetris border (see page 32), it's aniseed-scented seed pods were the main attraction. Sweet cicely is a hardy perennial member of the carrot family. It can be found in the wild in the north of England, and in northeast Scotland it's said to vie with cow parsley to be the star of the hedgerow. It's a pretty plant for a kitchen garden or wild border, with clusters of white flowers that appear in spring and early summer. This herb is attractive to bees and other beneficial pollinators in spring and early summer. In fact, sweet cicely's flowers are some of the first to be available for nectar-loving insects each year.

GROW ⬭ H 0.5-1.2M; W 0.1-0.5M

Sweet cicely grows up to 1.2m (4ft) tall. It prefers partial shade and well-drained humus-rich soil. That said, I have two plants in my garden and the one in the shadier position isn't quite as happy. Once established sweet cicely self-seeds readily. Propagate by seed or by division in spring or autumn. Sow seeds directly into a well-prepared seedbed in autumn, watering freely and thinning the plants to 25cm (10in) intervals as they grow. If necessary, transplant new plants in the spring. Or keep the seed for 4 weeks in the refrigerator and then sow it into pots in spring, allowing just one seed per pot. Plant outside after all risk of frost has passed.

CARE

Sweet cicely self-seeds so deadhead regularly if you don't want more plants. Cut back after flowering to encourage fresh growth.

PESTS & DISEASES

None of note.

HARVEST & STORAGE

Pick the leaves and young stems from spring until late summer, but choose fresh, tender growth. You can collect the seeds while still green in summer, or wait for them to turn brown. The roots are best dug up when the foliage dies back in autumn.

HOME REMEDIES

The plant can be used as a wood polish to create a deep lustre on wooden surfaces. Take a handful each of leaves and unripe green seeds, crush into a paste and rub on wood. It buffs up to produce a glossy finish, especially on oak. The leaves and stems of sweet cicely can be boiled with cabbage or sprouts to reduce the gassy side-effects of those vegetables. Drinking sweet cicely tea or taking a tincture or lozenge will help with indigestion or wind.

CULINARY USES

The leaves and seedpods taste like a mild-flavoured liquorice. Sweet cicely seeds and leaves can be used as a substitute for sugar, both fresh and dried. The leaves can be steeped to flavour custards and the leaves and/or about 10 seeds can be added to stewing fruit to reduce the amount of sugar needed. The stems can be candied. Try steeping some sweet cicely (stems, leaves, flowers, seeds – the lot) in vodka for a few weeks to make a great anise schnapps. Sweet cicely leaves can also be used to make a delicious herbal tea. The stems can also be used to freshen breath and to flavour cocktails and drinks, a little like a flavoured cocktail stick.

CATMINT

(NEPETA SPP.)

I've grown catmint for as long as I've had my cat, Syd. From the first season the plant flowered, almost as if Syd had read a set of instructions, she dutifully sniffed it, rolled in it and then gallivanted around the garden in pure ecstasy.

The frothy clouds of purple flowers and silvery foliage of catmint create much the same effect as lavender (see page 78), which is good news if you have heavy, moist soil and can't grow lavender. Bees love its nectar-rich flowers.

GROW ✧ H 0.5–1M; W 0.1–0.5M

Catmint is happy in sun or partial shade. *Nepeta* 'Six Hills Giant' is a good cultivar for a border. However, there are also more compact varieties that are better suited to containers, such as *N. nervosa* 'Blue Moon' and *N. racemosa* 'Snowflake', as well as the dwarf *N. racemosa* 'Little Titch'. *N. glechoma* 'Variegata' trails perfectly for hanging baskets. Nepeta cataria is commonly known as catnip, but it isn't as pretty, so other nepeta species are more commonly grown (catmints), which still are loved by cats but provide more interest for gardeners too. If you don't want the neighbourhood's cats in your garden don't grow it!

CARE

'Six Hills Giant', which is the cultivar I grow, flops and looks a little thin in the middle. The answer to this problem is to give the plant the "Chelsea chop" in early summer. Named after the famous RHS Chelsea Flower Show that takes place in London in May, the idea is to cut back two-thirds of the plant to promote more compact growth. Admittedly, the process delays flowering, but I've never minded the late-summer blooms – and Syd hasn't complained either. You will also need to cut back faded flowers and stems at the end of the season, ready for new growth in the spring. Divide the plant in spring or autumn.

PESTS & DISEASES

Slugs and powdery mildew.

HARVEST & STORAGE

Pick stems with young leaves as the flowers start to bloom, then spread out to dry.

HOME REMEDIES

Containing nepetalactone, which naturally relaxes the body, catmint tea helps insomnia and relieves headaches. To make the tea, mix dried flowers with boiling water then add honey and a squeeze of lemon juice. Adding a dash of catmint tea to soups, stews and sauces is said to help digestion.

Catmint-infused water can be used as a hair conditioner to help detangle and cure split ends. Oil infused with catmint can be used as an insect repellent.

CULINARY USES

You could eat young, tender leaves in salad – used sparingly – it's more a flavour than a 'salad' leaf.

NIGELLA

(NIGELLA SATIVA)

I was really eager to grow *Nigella sativa* for its delicious seeds, which are known as black cumin. I had thought that all nigella could be grown to harvest its seeds, but from a culinary perspective this particular species is the one you want. It's a pretty annual and the flower of this variety is white rather than blue, so it sparkles in the twilight.

GROW H: 0.1-0.5M; W 0.1-0.5M

This annual is worth growing successionally. Sowing seeds each month from spring (after all risk of frost has passed) until late summer will give you plenty of flowers for a longer season, not to mention a great supply of seeds to harvest. Choose a sunny spot and make sure the soil is free-draining. Nigella is a useful plant for containers, too, with its wispy foliage and delicate flowers providing a lovely contrast with more structural plants like agastache and echinacea that it grows in front of in my Tetris border.

CARE

Nigella demands very little in the way of TLC once it gets going but it will appreciate a feed in spring before growth begins – comfrey liquid feed is ideal (see page 96).

PESTS & DISEASES

None of note.

HARVEST & STORAGE

Once the flowers have faded, the gorgeous spiked seedpods will form. Either let them dry on the plant or pick them off and place them in a paper bag to dry out completely. Once the seedpods are dried, rub the bag in your hands to break up the dried pods and release the seeds, then snip off a small corner of the bag and pour out the seeds into a sieve – the idea being the crushed pod will stay inside the bag. Let the seeds dry thoroughly before storing in an airtight container.

HOME REMEDIES

Steep the seeds in water and add a little honey to help the digestive system, soothe stomach pains and ease wind and bloating.

The seeds are known to repel certain insects and can also be used like mothballs. I've read that the powdered seed can be used to remove head lice.

CULINARY USES

Nigella seeds have many delicious uses in dishes that call for a tangy, bitter flavour, especially breads. The seeds can also be ground and added to water to create a gel that can be used as an egg replacement in gluten-free and flour-free baking.

OREGANO

(ORIGANUM SPP.)

I can't do without oregano. Fresh or dried, this herb is a real winner when added to tomato-based dishes, homemade pizza and more besides. Oregano was the gateway herb for my son: he used to be indignant that I had added "bits" to red sauce, but enjoying the flavour and finding it not so "horrible" after all, these days he's resigned to picking oregano and other herbs to add to our homecooked meals, including red sauce, quiches, scones and anything else I can convince him to try. I was excited to find *Origanum syriacum*, or za'atar oregano, at one of the open days at Jekka McVicar's herb farm. It looks a bit more shrubby than the usual low-growing oregano and it tastes a bit more complex than its common cousin – a blend of thyme, marjoram and oregano. I've since discovered that it grows wild in the mountains of Lebanon, where it can reach up to 1m (3¼ft) in height, and it is the main herb in za'atar, a herb mix commonly used by the Lebanese people in their food. According to Kew's Millennium Seed Bank, za'atar oregano is an important crop as far as economics is concerned. Extensively harvested in the wild, it's on the endangered list, so it's well worth tracking down and growing this perennial plant as well as, or as an alternative to, the common variety of oregano.

GROW ⬳ H 0.5-1M; W 0.5-1M

Oregano likes full sun but can put up with some shade. It's happy in anything from poor to normal compost, as long as it's well-draining. Sow seeds in seed trays or directly in a container. Bring in under cover in the winter, somewhere with light, to protect them.

CARE

While oregano won't appreciate drying out completely, it doesn't need too much in the way of regular watering. Trim periodically to encourage new growth and help the plant keep its shape.

PESTS & DISEASES

Whitefly, powdery mildew and spider mites.

HARVEST & STORAGE

Pick leaves as needed and pick flowers in late summer. They can be used fresh or dried.

HOME REMEDIES

You can make a mild tea with oregano to aid sleep and ease stomach pains and sea sickness. A few drops of oregano-infused oil under your tongue can help soothe headaches, sore muscles, insect bites, toothache, arthritis and mild burns. Put equal measures of dried oregano leaves and oil in a jar with a sealed lid. Carefully place the jar in a saucepan of hot water to help the oregano to release its natural oil and leave in a sunny window for 2 weeks, shaking the jar every day. Strain the oil into a sterilized jar and store in a cool dark place.

CULINARY USES

To get the most flavour, finely chop and add it to food towards the end of cooking. If you're growing za'atar oregano, pick and dry the flowers and leaves, then crush them into a fine powder, which is very strong. To make the za'atar spice mix, combine powdered oregano with ground sumac, ground sesame seeds and salt.

SHISO PERILLA

(PERILLA FRUTESCENS)

This plant has been one of my surprise successes. The dense columns of deep-purple leaves with a bronze-green underside provide a beautiful foil for the soft pinks and purples in my borders. I'm not alone in recognizing the ornamental potential of this plant – the Victorians incorporated it in their much-loved bedding schemes, making the most of its dark foliage to set off pansies and begonias. A more modern champion of this plant is the ingenious hort-guru Alys Fowler. She grows it as a useful microgreen and suggests saving the seeds to ensure a steady supply.

GROW ☞ H 0.1-0.5M; W 0.1-0.5M

Plant it in a sunny spot with well-drained soil. It's easy to grow from seed sown indoors in spring. *Shisho perilla* does self-seed, so growing it in containers will prevent the plant taking over your garden.

CARE

Pinch out the tips to encourage fresh new growth. However, Alys warns, and I agree, that the slugs seems to love it when the plant is young and tender, so remain vigilant.

PESTS & DISEASES

Slugs and snails.

HARVEST & STORAGE

Harvest the young tender leaves and store them in the refrigerator on a sheet of kitchen paper. Dry the leaves for tea by spreading them out in the sun on a rack/stand.

HOME REMEDIES

Make a tea from the dried leaves to help ease sickness and fight colds.

CULINARY USES

Alys recommends using red shiso for pickling things (mostly turnips) as it dyes them a pink colour. She also suggests using it as an alternative to seaweed when wrapping sushi rice, adding it to summer rolls and using it as a garnish for fish dishes, particularly if they are curried.

Alys pointed me in the direction of a shiso soda, which resulted in some delicious recipes that require the leaves to be cold-steeped in a sweetened lime juice or watermelon juice and then the mixture to be carbonated.

Shisho leaves can be combined with Japanese rice vinegar to create a "drinking vinegar". Simply put 100g (3½oz) shiso leaves and 200ml (7fl oz) water in a saucepan and simmer for 5 minutes. Let cool for 5 minutes and then strain the liquid into a separate saucepan. Add 200ml (7oz) Japanese rice vinegar and 200g (7fl oz) sugar and simmer for just under a minute. Let cool and then transfer to a sterilized jar, where it will keep for up to 1 month. To use the drinking vinegar, dilute with sparkling water or try one part shiso vinegar to four parts ginger beer.

HERBS & SPICES

PARSLEY

(PETROSELINUM CRISPUM)

My grandmother used to grow curly parsley in vibrant green little clumps that edged the path of her vegetable garden. While it looked lovely, I must admit I didn't enjoy eating it. Perhaps we didn't pick the fresh, young growth because I remember the texture being tough and chewy. Worse still, I seem to recall that small slugs lurked ominously in the frills and only became visible when they were on your plate.

These days I like parsley (though only the flat-leaved variety – some scars are hard to heal) and I grow it in pots near the kitchen door, where it's easy to pick. There are some great large-leaved varieties available, like *Petroselinum hortense* 'Gigante di Napoli', which to my mind are the best ones to grow for taste, aesthetics and bountiful harvests.

GROW ✆ H 0.1-0.5M; W 0.1-0.5M

Parsley seeds are notoriously slow to germinate, so don't be despondent if yours take anything up to 4 weeks to get going. Give them plenty of warmth (bottom heat) if you're growing in pots on a windowsill or wait for the soil to warm up if you're sowing directly in the ground, and keep the faith. If this isn't for you, opt for plug plants. For a winter supply of parsley, cover outdoor plants in a cloche or bring indoors.

CARE

Water and feed regularly. The secret to keeping the leaves tender and lush is constant picking. If you want to prevent the plant setting seed, remove some of the flowering stems as they appear between midsummer and mid-autumn, but leave a few of the stems on the plant as bees and butterflies love the flowers. Snip off yellowing leaves to keep the plant looking good.

PESTS & DISEASES

Carrot fly and celery leaf miner.

HARVEST & STORAGE

To harvest, cut off stems close to the base, working from the outside in. Use the leaves fresh, freeze or dry them, though the flavour of dried parsley doesn't last long, perhaps up to 2 months.

HOME REMEDIES

Parsley tea has a diuretic action, helps with digestion and is calming. You can mash parsley into a paste and apply it to insect stings and bites.

CULINARY USES

Use parsley to flavour butter, cheese and oil.

ROSEMARY

(ROSMARINUS OFFICINALIS)

A few weeks ago, my editor Sophie and I were excited to see a full-page advert in a magazine for bottled rosemary water. It was a simple message designed to appeal to a health-conscious tribe. From my point of view, it was even better than that: why buy something that is so easy to make yourself? I'd wager that rosemary is one of those herbs that pretty much everyone's grown in their garden or on their windowsill at some point. It's certainly one of a few must-have herbs that I use in my kitchen on almost a daily basis. Depending on the space you have, there's a type of rosemary to suit most positions, whether neat and compact, upright, creeping or cascading. I chose the latter, picking a cultivar that forms bushy stems that resemble foxtails, hence its name, *Rosmarinus officinalis* 'Foxtail'. I bought it from Jekka McVicar, my friend and herb guru, who recommends it for containers or walls where it can happily spill over the edges. Out of the 30 varieties Jekka grows in her UK-based Herbetum, 'Green Ginger' is the variety she tells me she wouldn't be without. She loves its upright habit and its flavour (warm ginger combined with rosemary), which she uses with vegetables or finely chops and adds to pasta dough.

GROW ❤ H 0.5–1M; W 0.5–1M

Thinking about rosemary's native climate in the Mediterranean will give you an idea of the sort of conditions it prefers: hot and dry. While it will tolerate a small amount of shade, it'll be much happier in at least 6 hours of sunshine a day.

CARE

If you're growing rosemary in a container, let the soil dry out before giving it a good soaking. Once the rosemary has flowered, feed it with a balanced fertilizer. If severe frosts are predicted, move container-grown plants somewhere sheltered or cover with horticultural fleece. Cut back stems when the flowers fade to keep the plant compact and healthy. Take semi-ripe cuttings in late summer.

PESTS & DISEASES

Frost is the main issue – it will cause die-back on any affected stems. Rosemary beetle can pose something of a dilemma because it's a beautiful creature but it will decimate your plant, so as soon as you see it, remove it and dispose of it.

HARVEST & STORAGE

Rosemary can be harvested all year – the flowers too. In fact, as with all herbs, the more you pick, the happier the plant will be. Think of it as giving your plant a weekly short-back-and-sides. You can use the herb fresh or dried. The stems freeze well.

HOME REMEDIES

Jekka suggests that rosemary tea is a brilliant morning pick-me-up. All you need is a freshly picked stem, and off you go. It is said to help digestion and is good for mood and memory.

CULINARY USES

You can make rosemary bitters by steeping several rosemary sprigs and the entire peel of one grapefruit in a jar, covered in vodka, for 3 weeks. To make a zingy savoury rub, combine salt, chopped rosemary and lemon zest. Rosemary can also be used to infuse a vinegar or oil and, of course, water.

HERBS & SPICES

CLARY SAGE

(SALVIA HORMINUM & SALVIA VIRIDIS VAR. COMATA)

I love the mix of pink and purple flowers you have with clary sage, though, technically speaking, the "flowers" are actually bracts or modified leaves – the actual flowers are tiny and quite easy to miss.

Clary sage worked really well in my Tetris border (see page 32), even though it mingled with its neighbours in a rather over-familiar fashion – think of it as being like an airplane passenger who hogs the armrest. That said, its laid-back habit is actually quite a welcome characteristic as the plant can cover a substantial area and looks truly eye-catching.

Clary sage looks stunning when planted en masse. If possible, grow a few plants together or, perhaps, fill a decent-sized container with them. Pollinators love the colour of clary sage, and the foliage is aromatic, which is always a plus.

GROW ⬤ H 0.5-1M; W 0.1-0.5M

Sow seeds in spring or buy young plants. Choose a sunny or semi-shaded spot and make sure the soil is well-draining. This annual plant merrily self-seeds, so allow it to do this to ensure new plants next year, and if you have too many, just share them with friends once the seedlings are big enough to dig up.

CARE

Deadhead to encourage more colourful stems.

PESTS & DISEASES

Powdery mildew, rust, whitefly, aphids and spider mites.

HARVEST & STORAGE

Pick stems with leaves and flowers to use fresh or dried.

HOME REMEDIES

An infusion of the leaves may be used as an antiseptic gargle for sore gums and throats.

Make clary sage oil by tearing fresh leaves into small pieces and filling a jar with them (the more you can fit in, the more potent the oil). Cover the leaves with warmed olive oil, seal the jar and let infuse for 3–4 days, then strain and transfer to a sterilized jar. If necessary, you can dilute the final strength of the oil by adding extra olive oil. Clary sage oil can be used for bathing or massaging, as a mood enhancer, to ease anxiety, to help with menstrual cramps, and as an antiseptic treatment for grazes and scratches. Mix it with a carrier oil, such as jojoba oil, and massage onto oily skin to help clear clogged pores, and soothe tired eyes by adding a few drops of oil to a flannel, which you then run under warm water to disperse the oil, and lay over closed eyes for about 5 minutes.

CULINARY USES

Clary sage seeds and leaves were once used to flavour and increase the alcohol content of liqueurs. It's sweet and floral, though leaves taste more bitter with age. Try making a jelly with the leaves or using them to flavour stews and omelettes.

SAGE

(SALVIA OFFICINALIS)

I don't think I'm going out on a limb when I say that common sage isn't the sexiest plant to choose for your garden. While I'm not a fan of describing plants as "sexy", it sums up the issue that I think some folk have with sage. To my mind, however, sage is a massively underrated herb. I realize it doesn't have flashy colourful stems or a long flowering season (in fact, I can't remember mine ever flowering, though this could be because I'm always snipping it), yet it has a totally winning habit: a pleasing mound of faintly hairy leaves that flutter in the gentlest breeze.

There are several different varieties of sage that are determined by their leaf colour: plain silvery green, two-toned purple and green and variegated yellow and green, as well as a mixture of all three colours. I lean towards the demure silvery green and purple-tinged leaves because they are brilliant supporting-cast members for the diva-like plants that demand centre stage in your planting schemes. Sage plants can tie a border or container display together effortlessly.

Sage has a savoury fragrance and a delicious flavour. It flowers in midsummer and is evergreen, too. So the next time you're in the nursery and you spot a humble pot of soft, green aromatic leaves, don't make the mistake of thinking it looks a bit boring, just grab it.

GROW ◐ H 0.5-1M; W 0.5-1M

Sage will thrive in moist or well-drained soil in sunshine or a bit of shade. It's a fairly robust plant so can cope with being at the front of a border. Grow *Salvia officinalis tricolour* for a medley of pink, white and green, *S. purpurescens* for purple, and *S. aura* for yellow leaves.

CARE

Young plants are the best way to start growing sage, though you can sow seeds if you're patient. Water during warm, dry spells but be careful not to overwater. If you're growing sage in a container, raising the pot up on "pot feet" during the winter is a good idea to further improve drainage. Prune after flowering for shape and new growth. Protect from harsh frosts during the winter with a layer of horticultural fleece. Take softwood cuttings in early summer (see page 22).

PESTS & DISEASES

Powdery mildew, rosemary beetle and capsid bug.

HARVEST & STORAGE

Pick young, fresh leaves year round. They can be used fresh or dried.

HOME REMEDIES

Sage tea can soothe headaches, coughs, colds and rheumatism. It also works well when applied to insect bites. Sage is said to improve your memory.

CULINARY USES

Infuse fresh leaves in white wine, cider vinegar, oil or honey. You can make a sensational infused sugar, too. The dried leaves can be combined with coarse salt to make a sage salt seasoning.

You can make individual tinctures from each of the bitters ingredients and then add them to the vodka one at a time in order to control the flavour. Remember, you need a concentrated flavour to add to cocktails or sparkling water, so expect the bitters to be strong and punchy in undiluted form (see pages 40–43).

STEVIA

(STEVIA REBAUDIANA)

Jekka McVicar introduced me to this plant. She's been cultivating and championing stevia for years because, well, it's rather incredible that you can grow your own sugar substitute. Stevia is native to South America, where it's been used as a sweetener for centuries. Given that, it's quite surprising that stevia hasn't caught on quicker around the rest of the world. I can't imagine what forces might be at work to keep this calorie- and carbohydrate-free natural sweetener under the radar. Stevia is a brilliant herb. It has started to be used worldwide by those who seek out alternatives to sugar and sugary snacks. Its leaves are said to be 10–15 times sweeter than sugar, while stevia extract is a mind-blowing 300 times sweeter. There are some good websites and blogs online that discuss stevia and offer guidelines for using it. I never tire of teasing my gorgeous eight-year-old son by asking if he wants sugar in his tea (anything sweet rocks for an eight-year-old)… and then adding a green leaf. I fear the joke has worn a little thin, but I can't help it.

GROW ⬱ H 0.1-5M; W 0.1-0.5M

Choose a sunny spot to grow stevia, though it can have afternoon shade. I grow my plant in the glasshouse and the long hours of sunshine seem to suit it. Stevia isn't particularly fussy about soil, though free-draining soil is preferable.

CARE

Stevia is a tender perennial. If you're growing it outside, bring it inside over the winter. The stems will die down during the winter, but come spring the plant will produce roots with shoots that can be potted up. Water regularly but don't worry too much about feeding. Keep pinching the plant back to prevent flowering and encourage a bushy plant.

PESTS & DISEASES

Aphids, slugs and snails.

HARVEST & STORAGE

Harvest the whole plant in summer once the buds form but before the flowers bloom – once it has flowered the whole plant has a bitter aftertaste. Harvest in the morning when the leaves have the highest sugar content.

HOME REMEDIES

Stevia helps reduce blood sugar levels and fights cavities. In other words, it helps to avoid the issues associated with consuming too much sugar, though, I'm bound to say, only if you are controlling the rest of your diet. A tincture or tea made with stevia will help strengthen bones.

CULINARY USES

You can use fresh or dried stevia leaves to flavour hot drinks. Another way to use stevia in a variety of drinks and dishes is to make it into a syrup – 1 teaspoon of stevia syrup is as sweet as 1 cup (180g/6 ¼oz) of sugar. You can't use stevia as a substitute for sugar in most baking recipes because it doesn't have the other attributes of sugar. However, you can grind dried stevia into a white powder and use it as you would sugar for non-baked desserts, though be warned, stevia doesn't have the same bulk as sugar so a bit of experimentation is necessary.

THYME

(THYMUS SPP.)

Thyme has a long history of use in natural medicine. In Ancient Egypt it was used for embalming, and over the centuries it has been thought to ward off the plague, soothe respiratory problems and even cure shyness. Modern herbalists value thyme's antibacterial, insecticidal and, some believe, antifungal properties. Having only ever grown thyme for its attractive, low-growing habit and delicious savoury flavour, I was surprised to learn how many benefits this unassuming herb offers.

Thyme is a versatile plant: its leaf colour can vary from dark green to golden yellow, as well as variegated, and its growth habit ranges from ground-hugging to upright. It's also evergreen, so it's well worth finding thyme a small space in your plot.

GROW ⟠ H 0.1-0.5M; W 0.1-0.5M

Grow thyme in the ground or in a container. While it doesn't need too much in the way of water, don't let the soil dry out during hot summer months. Once planted, mulch with some horticultural grit to protect the leaves from being splashed with mud. You can sow from seed in spring, though young plants are probably an easier, better bet. *Thymus serpyllum* 'Annie Hall' is compact; *Thymus pulegioides* 'Archer's Gold' has lovely yellow foliage; grow *Thymus herba-barona* and *Thymus pulegioides* 'Foxley' for a delicate cream-edge.

CARE

Move pot-grown plants out of the rain as thyme won't appreciate being left to luxuriate in soggy soil; in fact, it will rot. Feed once a week with a liquid fertilizer. To keep sprigs fresh and tender, divide the plant after 3 years, when it is most likely to have become a bit woody.

PESTS & DISEASES

Mealybugs.

HARVEST & STORAGE

You can snip leaves all year round, though they will taste best during the growing season. Whenever you harvest sprigs, take the opportunity to tidy up the plant's compact shape and keep it neat. Regular harvesting helps prevent the plant becoming too woody. The leaves can be used fresh or dried for later use.

HOME REMEDIES

Fascinatingly, thyme oil was used to medicate bandages before the invention of modern antibiotics. A tincture can be used to treat acne. Use finely chopped fresh thyme or dried thyme as a substitute for salt to help lower cholesterol. To soothe a cough or sore throat, either drink thyme tea or combine a teaspoon each of dried thyme, oregano and mint in a bowl of boiling water and inhale the steam.

CULINARY USES

Using fresh thyme in dishes will protect against food-borne illnesses. Thyme makes deliciously flavoured salt, vinegar and oil. You can also infuse honey with dried thyme and use it to sweeten drinks or in baking. Thyme is one of the herbs used to flavour the aromatic Bénédictine liqueur, which was developed in 19th-century France. You can make a thyme martini by mixing 3 parts citrus juice, 2 parts vodka and 1 part thyme syrup.

SZECHUAN PEPPER

(ZANTHOXYLUM SCHINIFOLIUM)

I consulted my lovely friend Mark Diacono, the guru grower and "unusual edibles" evangelist, for advice about this plant. After all, he's the reason so many of us know that growing your own Szechuan pepper is possible in our mild climate. In fact, he's responsible for it becoming a bit of a thing… Mark says: "It is the plant I enjoy most throughout the year. Its leaves come early in spring and last until mid-winter when the final peppers are harvested, and I pause daily as I walk past to get the scent of its leaves on my fingers. Those tiny early leaves add a wonderful kick to salads and, when larger, they are great in stir-fries, mayo and many other recipes. Clusters of tiny flowers emerge in early summer. In midsummer, the flowers become tiny fruit, flipping from upturned flowers to hanging peppercorns."

GROW ⬯ H 3-4M; W 3-4M

Choose a sunny spot and don't worry about the soil, although you should avoid it becoming waterlogged. Add fertilizer when planting.

CARE

Water regularly, though it can cope with drought. Although this plant will grow to 6m (20ft) tall in time, it is easy to keep it under control either by pruning it (at any time of year, and into any shape you like), growing it in a container (which has the effect of bonsaiing it) or choose one of the naturally smaller varieties or Japanese pepper that grow more slowly to a diminutive fullness.

PESTS & DISEASES

Generally trouble free.

HARVEST & STORAGE

Szechuan peppercorns are commercially harvested when they've turned from green through purple-brown into a gloriously vibrant pink-red. You can pick them at any stage from these tiny green spheres to full-sized and vivid red in early July. Keen to enjoy the harvest, Mark picks a few handfuls of the early green peppercorns from a couple of his plants that grow in the most sheltered sunny spot. He says, "these intense, bright green peppercorns taste slightly metallic, in a good way, and have a freshness that, while not better, is certainly different to the red peppercorns, which can be picked any time between autumn and midwinter." Use the peppercorns fresh or dried or freeze them.

HOME REMEDIES

In some cultures, the numbing effect from these peppercorns has been used to soothe toothache, hence its colloquial name: the toothache tree.

CULINARY USES

I agree with Mark when he says "alongside the peppery flavour is a culinary sensation unlike any other: a gentle anaesthetizing that spreads across the lips and tongue. It's known as *ma la* in Szechuan cooking: the *ma* being the tingle, the *la* the peppery heat. It's delightfully addictive, and long thought in Szechuan Province to impart a spiritual lift. A few crushed green peppercorns usually find their way into my salad dressings or are used to make a marinade for a steak, and red peppercorns can be dried and ground to use as a spice."

HERBS & SPICES

FRUIT
&
VEG

Having grown fruit and vegetables for years, both on an allotment and in my garden, I was truly excited to have the chance to replace staple crops with more exotic varieties. It was a brilliant journey of new discoveries and I heartily encourage you to join me in doing the same – come rain, shine or freezing weather, I still love to sneak out to the greenhouse, open the door and breathe in the heady scent of the citrus plants.

JUNEBERRY

(AMELANCHIER SPP.)

I chose to grow *Amelanchier lamarckii* in my garden about 3 years ago when my rear neighbours chopped down their trees to reveal not only their house but also about 30 other windows of neighbouring houses. This was a bit distressing, to say the least, but my next-door neighbours on the right-hand side tried to be philosophical about it and we decided to plant our own trees in an effort to recreate some privacy. Today, I have two juneberry trees along the back fence in my garden and my neighbours have one.

Together, these three trees help to blur the boundaries and create the longest possible privacy screen. I'm thrilled we agreed to go with this type of tree (which can also be grown as a large shrub). It has beautiful blossom in the spring, followed by berries that appear, as its common name suggests, in early summer, and it finishes the year with a fiery display of autumn leaves. The tree is deciduous, but bare branches in winter are a small price to pay for the pleasure it provides for the rest of the year.

While researching this book, I was delighted to discover that the berries are edible. Up until this year, I haven't had a look-in at the berries; much like with cherries and currants, one day there's a bountiful crop and the next day there are just several plump-looking pigeons swaying precariously on the dainty juneberry branches. However, this summer my vigilance paid off and, though I did leave the pigeons a share, I managed to pick enough berries to freeze for use later on.

I also grow another variety, *A. alnifolia*, or 'Saskatoon Saskablue', which I positioned in a less accessible spot that wasn't clocked by the pigeons.

As I've already mentioned (see page 28), trees might seem a silly idea if you've only got a small garden, but they can actually provide height and interest, tricking the eye and expanding the sense of space. Juneberries are a great choice because they can be grown as a standard with a raised canopy that acts as a delicate screen. (For a small plot, avoid trees with a heavy lollipop canopy because the dense ball of branches and leaves will block a view or vista and abruptly halt the eyeline. You want your garden design to flow rather than appear jarring.)

GROW ⬙ H 4–8M; W 4–8M
This hardy specimen will cope in shade or full sun. However, for the best autumn colour, choose a sunny spot. It likes moist fertile soil that's free-draining.

CARE
Light pruning is all the tree really needs to keep it in the best of health. Remove damaged or crossing branches in winter or early spring.

PESTS & DISEASES
No problems.

HARVEST & STORAGE
Pick the berries when they are deep purple and ripe.

HOME REMEDIES
None of note.

CULINARY USES
The berries of Saskatoon Saskablue have very high levels of anthocyanins and antioxidants and they are also very rich in calcium and iron. The berries are good for making a jelly or jam.

For a wintry tipple, steep the berries in gin or vodka for a few months and then sweeten to taste with sugar syrup.

WILDLIFE BROWNIE POINTS
Juneberries provide insects with an early supply of nectar.

STRAWBERRY TREE

(ARBUTUS UNEDO)

I loved the strawberry tree in the garden of my childhood home because it reminded me of the type of lollipop trees that illustrators drew for children's books: a perfect round ball of leaves on top of a tall, straight stem.

To my mind, a strawberry tree is worth its weight in gold. It's evergreen, so there's foliage all year round, and autumn brings an extra treat with a dashing display of honey-scented white flowers and, more often than not, the odd fruit from last year's flowers. The taste of the fruit won't set your world on fire – they have a very delicate flavour that reminds me a little bit of figs – but their aesthetic appeal makes this tree deserving of being included.

I hadn't thought about growing a strawberry tree in my small urban garden because I already had two juneberry trees growing along the back fence. However, after playing around with the design, I felt sure that adding height towards the middle of the plot, rather than at the boundary, would make the space feel bigger and more interesting.

GROW ⬲ H 4-8M; W 4-8M

If you're growing it in a container, choose a good-sized pot that a young tree can grow into because it won't like to be disturbed. Strawberry trees like well-drained soil, so add some horticultural grit or sharp sand to the compost. Sun and warmth are essential; choose a sheltered position out of any potential frost pockets. This is a great specimen for city plots because it tolerates pollution.

CARE

This tree doesn't need too much in the way of pruning. Remove broken, diseased or crossing branches in late autumn or winter.

PESTS & DISEASES

Arbutus leaf spot.

HARVEST & STORAGE

Pick fruits in late autumn/early winter. Eat them straight away or use the fruit to make teas or liquor.

HOME REMEDIES

You can make a tea with the fresh fruit to use as a gargle for treating sore and irritated throats: put about 20g ($^3/_4$ oz) each of strawberry tree leaves and bramble leaves in a saucepan with enough water to cover the leaves in a saucepan and boil for 5 minutes. Remove from the heat and let steep for 10 minutes, then strain. Drink 2 cups of this tea a day for upset stomachs. You can also try making a tea with a few strawberries and some honey, lemon juice and cinnamon – a sort of hot toddy.

CULINARY USES

The fruit has a high pectin content and can be added to other fruit to make jams and preserves – I think "strawberry tree" or "arbutus" looks rather fancy on a label. The fruit is the main ingredient in the Portuguese tipple of choice, medronho, a type of strong brandy (*medronho* is the Portuguese word for the strawberry tree berries). You can combine strawberry tree fruit with vodka and sugar syrup, much in the way you'd make damson vodka or sloe gin (see pages 189 and 191), letting it macerate for about 6 months before drinking.

FRUIT & VEG

CHILLI

(CAPSICUM ANNUUM)

If you're not a chilli fan, I urge you to try growing them. You can enjoy more nuanced flavours from homegrown varieties and you can also pick the chillies before they reach their peak of heat if you don't want to have your socks blown off. There's lots of information available to help you choose which type of chilli to go for, including the Scoville Scale, which is the traditional measure for the heat of chillies. There are mild varieties, like 'Bishop's Crown'; hot ones, like 'Joe's Long Cayenne'; very hot ones, like 'Demon Red'; super-hot ones, like 'Prairie Fire'; and then there are ones that are (almost) too hot to handle, such as *Capsicum chinense* 'Bhut Jolokia'. So have some fun, choose a variety and see what you like.

GROW ☉ H 0.5-2M; W 0.1-0.5M

One of the many great things about chillies is that you can get going growing them as early as the start of the new year, which is good news if you're itching to get your botanical garden off to a flying start. Sowing early will mean, hopefully, that there's enough time at the other end of the season for the chillies to have ripened, which is important for the hottest types. The seeds will need a bit of heat, so either use a heated propagator with a lid or cover trays with a plastic bag. A sunny windowsill works well, too.

CARE

Water regularly; though it's actually good news if you're a little haphazard when it comes to watering chilli plants because keeping them a bit on the dry side stresses the plants and boosts the heat of the

chillies. Feed weekly once the first flowers appear. Pinch out tips to encourage healthy, bushy plants, and stake taller varieties. If growing indoors, open windows to ensure the plants are visited by pollinating insects.

PESTS & DISEASES

Aphids, whitefly and grey mould.

HARVEST & STORAGE

Use chillies fresh or string them up to dry for about 4 weeks. The drying process will enhance the flavour and also allow you to keep the dried seed to sow next year. Red chillies dry better than green.

Chillies contain a chemical called capsaicin that can produce a burning sensation when it comes into contact with mucous membranes. You might feel silly doing so, but wear gloves when harvesting or preparing chillies to prevent the capsaicin burning anything you touch.

You can roast whole chillies (green work well), slitting the ends a little to prevent them bursting, and then freeze them.

HOME REMEDIES

The same compound, capsaicin, that produces the burning heat of a chilli also causes blood vessels to relax, so it could help with high blood pressure. It's also thought to help migraines, boost circulation, induce a longer sleep and relieve blocked-up sinuses. There's also research to show it can lower the amount of insulin needed to reduce the body's blood sugar after a meal.

CONTINUED...

CULINARY USES

Infuse fresh or dried chillies in oil, chop up dried chillies and combine them with salt for a spicy seasoning or use fresh chillies to make delicious sweet chilli jam. Fresh chillies can be pickled to make preserved accompaniments for mezze platters – simply prick the chillies and then add them to an airtight jar with salt, white wine vinegar or water.

Dried red chillies can be used to create the traditional ingredient used in Mexican cooking to make red sauce for delicious dishes like huevos rancheros. For dried chillies, gently toast the fresh chillies to release their flavour – don't overdo it as it will make them bitter, around 30 seconds is probably enough, depending on their size. Grind the toasted chillies in a spice or coffee grinder, or go the old-fashioned route and use a pestle and mortar. Store the chilli powder in airtight jar in a cool, dark place or freeze. It'll keep for up to a year.

Until recently, I didn't realize that chilli powder isn't just powdered chillies. Created in Texas in the 1800s, chilli powder is actually a blend of chilli, cumin, oregano, black pepper (sometimes), dehydrated garlic and onions. Who knew? I'm going to experiment this winter to make my own blend of chilli powder because a big bowl of chilli after a cold, wintry walk is a tradition in my house.

You can also infuse chillies in vodka, tequila or sherry for a drink with a fiery kick – you'll need to slit the fresh chillies to help them sink into the liquid. If you chop up the chillies before adding them to the alcohol, remember, the finer you chop them up, the hotter the end result.

CITRUS

(CITRUS & FORTUNELLA)

If, like me, you thought that citrus trees were hard to grow without a big glasshouse or conservatory, then you're in for a treat. It turns out most varieties of lemon, orange and grapefruit will flourish in the UK, given the right care and attention. True, you'll need to bring them indoors over winter but other than that they're pretty low maintenance. If you don't have outdoor space, you can grow them indoors in a light sunny corner of a room.

During my research for this book, I was fascinated to learn that fossilized citrus leaves have been discovered in China's Yunnan Province, pointing to the fact that some form of citrus fruit was growing seven million years ago. It's only been in the last few thousand years that three key species – mandarins, pomelo and citron – were hybridized to create the oranges, lemons, grapefruit and limes that we're used to seeing on the supermarket shelves.

It's really rewarding to grow your own citrus trees. They have heavenly scented flowers, year-round glossy leaves and all kinds of weird and wonderful fruit. Before you know it, you'll be asking yourself why you've never tried growing citrus before.

GROW ✧ H 2.5-4M; W 1.5-2.5M

Given that South and East Asia is their native habitat, citrus trees prefer constant warm temperatures. As the summer weather in the UK is unpredictable, growing citrus in pots is the best option, allowing you to move the plants into the warmth during the colder months. Citrus are happy for their roots to be a little restricted; they won't complain as long as you provide them with a specialized compost (a mixture of three-quarters potting on compost and one-quarter crushed bark of the smallest grade).

CARE

Citrus really benefit from drying out and then being given a good soak, so don't overwater, or water little and often. This may seem counterintuitive, but watch for signs of drought and then water well. In winter, leave it about 8 weeks between each watering. As a very rough rule of thumb, citrus need watering each week (no more) in a very hot UK summer and no water at all during winter. A good way to check if the plant is sufficiently watered is to examine the fruit: they should be firm – the softer the fruit, the more likely the plant is to need watering.

Citrus plants are never dormant so they need feeding every month. The French king Louis XIV had his gardeners use sheep droppings soaked in water to nourish his lemons, but you can settle for a liquid feed with a high nitrogen content from spring until early autumn and a specialized winter feed from mid autumn to early spring.

Pruning is best done in early spring. Feel free to get scissor-happy if your citrus has become too spindly. Expect to curb its enthusiasm at least once over three or four seasons.

CONTINUED...

PESTS & DISEASES

Vine weevil, scale insects, greenfly and red spider mites.

HARVEST & STORAGE

Unlike most crops, citrus fruit won't continue to ripen or sweeten after they have been picked, so making sure the fruit is at its peak is key – a taste test is your best bet. Cut with secateurs and store for several weeks in the refrigerator. The great thing about citrus is that the fruit have their own growing cycle, and with some varieties you can have flowers and fruits at the same time. After harvesting, you can freeze the juice and zest separately (ice-cube trays work well) until required.

HOME REMEDIES

Apart from the obvious benefits of vitamin C, there are plenty of other uses for citrus. Lemon juice diluted in water can be applied as a disinfectant for minor wounds and lemon juice mixed with olive oil will nourish dry, brittle nails.

To make your own orange powder, dry orange peel for a few days and then use a food processor or blender to grind to a fine powder. Two teaspoons of orange powder can be mixed with 1 teaspoon each of oatmeal and bicarbonate of soda to create a face mask for oily skin or mix 1 tablespoon orange powder with 2 tablespoons of yogurt and apply on your face, washing off after 15 minutes to freshen and tone the skin.

For lime "caviar", dry the pith and then grind it with a spice or coffee grinder or mortar and pestle to make a powder. You can add little balls of the "caviar" to champagne or crush it and add to gin.

CULINARY USES

Steep a slice or two of your favourite citrus fruit in boiling water for a therapeutic tea. Citrus can also be used to make candied peel, marmalade and to flavour oils, vinegars and liquor.

I suggest growing the following citrus for culinary use:

- Buddha's hands (*Citrus medica* var. *sarcodactylis*): I couldn't resist trying this incredibly bizarre-looking lemon. It's hard to get hold of the fruit so growing my own seemed a great idea. The fruit is practically all rind, though slightly sweet rather than bitter, so it's absolutely perfect for making candied peel or marmalade. It also makes a lovely flavoured vodka and looks great in cocktails.

- Horned Bitter Orange (*Citrus aurantium* 'Canaliculata'): This is a ribbed fruit that's a good substitute for making Seville orange marmalade.

- Round kumquat (*Fortunella japonica*): Sizewise, this and the calamondin (see page 175) are ideal for growing indoors. Sweet, juicy and slightly tart, the fruit can be eaten straight off the tree or served between meals as a palate cleanser. Soak the fruit in brandy and brown sugar to make a delicious liqueur.

- Yuzu (*Citrus junos*): Containing three times the amount of vitamin C as a lemon, this fruit has a complex flavour and is loved by foodies. It's a cross between a lime and a grapefruit – quite sharp and very refreshing. The juice can be added to hot baths as a skin toner.

FRUIT & VEG

CALAMONDIN

(CITRUS × MICROCARPA)

I used to think these bonsai citrus were purely ornamental. However, this little tree produces delicious dinky edible fruit that look and taste like the offspring of an illicit liaison between a kumquat and a mandarin. More than that, calamondin is an absolute workhorse that doesn't demand much in the way of care, yet produces a winning combination of evergreen leaves, scented flowers and a harvestable crop all year round – more often than not, all at the same time. Take it from me, this is great news – once you've tasted calamondin-flavoured vodka, you won't want your supply of fruit to run out. So why not share the love and give a friend a calamondin tree? They are traditionally given as gifts during Chinese New Year because they signify good luck.

GROW ⬙ H 0.5-1M; W 0.5-1M

Native to China, the calamondin will thrive outside in a cool climate in free-draining but nutrient-rich soil. It can reach up to 4m (13ft) tall. I must confess, I've kept mine in my very sunny kitchen, where it seems perfectly at home, however, if you can't find a spot with plenty of light indoors, keep it outside once all risk of frost has passed. Calamondin can cope with shade, but you'll get more fruit in full sun. To plant, choose a loam-based potting compost, and add a few handfuls of grit for drainage. It can be propagated via seedings or by taking softwood cuttings in the spring or semi-ripe cuttings in the summer, or bud-grafted onto sour orange rootstock.

CARE

Like all citrus (see page 171), calamondin is drought tolerant but would prefer not to be deprived of a drink. As you'll most likely be growing this plant in a container, give it a good soak every week or so, as opposed to watering little and often. During the summer, feed the plant every couple of weeks with a citrus feed and, if the mood takes you, it'll thank you for a daily misting, too.

PESTS & DISEASES

Typical glasshouse pests, such as whitefly, red spider mites, scale insects and mealybugs, are less of an issue if your calamondin is grown outdoors. However, if you're growing it indoors, keep the leaves free of dust to prevent problems.

HARVEST & STORAGE

To avoid damaging the stems, use scissors to snip off the fruit. Go for the yellow to yellow-orange fruit as they have the strongest flavour; when the fruit is bright orange, it's overripe and not as pungent.

HOME REMEDIES

Put a few slices of the fruit in a bowl, pour over 1 litre (1¾ pints) boiling water and let cool. The infused liquid can be used as a final rinse after washing your hair, as an alternative to deodorant and to soothe any irritation caused by insect bites.

CULINARY USES

Calamondin is cultivated for its juice throughout South East Asia. However, you'd need a fair few of our bonsai trees to get enough fruit to make even a shot-glass full of juice! The sharp-tasting fruits are ideal for making syrups and flavouring alcohol. I've had it on good authority (the owners of the fabulous Citrus Centre nursery in West Sussex, England) that the fruit can be used to make the most delicious marmalade, though you may need to bulk up the quantity of fruit with kumquats or limes.

SAMPHIRE

(CRITHMUM MARITIMUM)

Whether you're growing this salty sea veg (as we like to call it in our household) on a balcony, a windowsill or in the garden, it's one of those plants that will bring you total pleasure when you get to harvest it.

Unless you live on the coast and have found a wild supply of samphire from which to forage, most likely you'll need to buy it from a fishmonger or, if you're lucky, a supermarket. Alas, in my experience, samphire is never stocked in huge quantities, meaning it's often sold out when you want to buy it. This may explain why I got such a buzz from growing my own this year, and I'm looking forward to having more plants next year to provide me with plenty of the tender tips for pickling.

GROW ⟳ H 0.1-0.5M; W 0.1-0.5M

As you might imagine, given its natural habitat, samphire needs sandy, free-draining soil and a good deal of sunlight.

CARE

Keep plants moist by watering them with salt water (made by adding 1 teaspoon sea salt to 1 pint water).

PESTS & DISEASES

No issues.

HARVEST & STORAGE

Pick fresh growth between early and late summer, after which time the shoots become woody. Samphire is a cut-and-come-again plant, but patience is required as new growth takes about a month to reach a harvestable size. Be sure to leave some tips to flower in late summer so that they can produce seeds in early autumn, then collect the seeds or leave the plant to self-seed to provide next year's plants.

HOME REMEDIES

The benefits of samphire are many, including helping your immune system and digestion, improving bone health and even aiding sleep.

CULINARY USES

Samphire makes a salty snack. Nibble it fresh or lightly steamed or pickle the shoots with vinegar and your choice of spices.

CUCUMBER

(CUCUMIS SATIVUS)

Cucumbers are great fun to grow whether you've got a garden or not. There are varieties that are happy in the great outdoors as well as those that will romp away indoors, either in a glasshouse or on a bright windowsill. Homegrown cucumbers really do taste much better, though the skins can sometimes be thicker. I opted for *Cucumis sativus* 'Crystal Lemon', a cute round yellow cucumber that grows outdoors, looks gorgeous, has a sweet mild flavour and is super juicy – great for making the face toner for which I had it earmarked. This variety is also a late-fruiter, which is always appreciated once the boom of high-summer crops has passed. I recommend trying 'La Diva', a great outdoor variety and 'Femdan' and 'Zeina' for growing indoors, too.

GROW ✏ H 1.5-2M; W 0.1-0.5M

Cucumbers are easy to get going from seed: sow indoors from late winter to early spring or outdoors from mid spring (as long as the weather is warm) to early summer. Whether you've chosen to grow your cucumber in a pot, grow bag or border, make sure it has plenty of well-rotted organic matter in the soil mix from seedling stage onward. You can train cucumbers up a wigwam or along a trellis.

CARE

To encourage healthy growth, pinch out the growing tip when there are about seven leaves on the plant. Water regularly and feed during the growing season.

PESTS & DISEASES

Whitefly, powdery mildew and cucumber mosaic virus.

HARVEST & STORAGE

Remove the fruit using a knife. If you're planning to juice your cucumbers, you might want to leave them until they are quite big before harvesting them.

HOME REMEDIES

Being so full of water and the same pH as our skin, cucumbers make excellent facial toners (see page 44). They're also soothing to eyes, burns and irritated skin. Drinking cucumber juice is great for helping skin look bright and healthy, thanks to its high levels of silica and high water content.

CULINARY USES

Cucumbers are delicious when used to make a chilled soup and they are great as a healthy snack.

DWARF QUINCE

(CYDONIA OBLONGA 'LESKOVAC')

I will go to almost any length to avoid spending the ludicrously huge amounts of money necessary to buy quince in the shops. When I spotted a quince tree in a front garden in my local neighbourhood, I thought nothing of knocking on the door to ask if I could be so rude as to "scrump" some of their quinces. (Can you scrump fruit other than apples?) Thankfully, the owners of this tree were more than happy for me to pick some of their fruit in return for some membrillo (quince paste). I was thrilled to discover a dwarf quince variety in my research for the book.

GROW ⬤ H 1.5-2M; W 0.05M

This dwarf quince is hardy but needs plenty of sun and a bit of shelter. While this variety reaches up to 2m (6½ft) in height, you can restrict it a little by the size of the container you choose. It's self-fertile so you'll only need to find room for one tree. Patience is required though, because it'll take a few years to reach a size when it will bear fruit. However, once it starts, you'll be rewarded with golden pear-shaped quince each autumn. It's well worth the wait.

CARE

Feed and water container plants regularly. Patio quince trees will require little pruning. Prune the tips of the main branches by one-third in winter.

PESTS & DISEASES

Generally free from pests and diseases.

HARVEST & STORAGE

Pick the fruit in autumn.

HOME REMEDIES

Quince can be boiled, baked or made into a syrup to relieve nausea and vomiting. Quince juice is helpful in the treatment of cardiovascular diseases, respiratory ailments, anaemia and asthma. When gargled, the juice treats mouth ulcers, bad breath and sore throats.

CULINARY USES

The fruit needs to be cooked to reduce the tannins and make the flavour more mellow and perfumed. Poach the fruit and serve it with yogurt or make it into a set paste, better known as membrillo. Quince jelly and marmalade is also delicious. You can add quince juice to gin to make a delicious drink.

FIG

(FICUS CARICA)

Who wouldn't delight at the idea of picking and eating a fig fresh from the tree? I love figs, but until recently I hadn't considered growing them in the UK. However, the UK's summers are getting warmer and it's possible to grow figs in most areas where the temperature doesn't fall below -15°C (5°F) in winter, and you can always grow them in a heated glasshouse if you're in a colder region. There are lots of varieties of fig to choose from. I chose 'Brown Turkey', which is widely available and pretty reliable, too.

GROW ⬙ H 2.5-4M; W 2.5-4M

You can grow a fig in the ground or a large container. Ideally, position it up against a wall as this provides shelter and extra warmth, plus you can have fun training it up the wall or against a trellis. If you're planting in the ground, it's a good idea to restrict the roots by providing a physical barrier (paving slabs or bricks around the edges of the wider-than-usual planting hole are fine); this will encourage the plant to produce fruit instead of putting its energy into leaf growth. Figs handle the cold well when they're in a border but you will need to provide winter shelter for pot-grown plants.

CARE

Figs need to be watered regularly, especially during hot weather, to prevent fruits dropping prematurely. However, too much water or erratic watering will make the fruit split so try to stick to watering little and often, especially if the plant is in a container. Border-grown plants should be fed weekly while the fruits are developing, whereas it's best to start feeding container-grown plants in the spring. Repot plants that have outgrown their containers in winter

– figs will usually need repotting after about 3 years. Remove small figs or a second crop that appears in winter as the fruits won't survive the cold weather, and if they do, they aren't likely to ripen. Prune older bare branches in late winter. To encourage a healthy plant, aim to remove about a quarter of its older branches over a period of 2 to 3 years.

PESTS & DISEASES

Birds and, if growing under glass, scale insects and spider mites.

HARVEST & STORAGE

If you live in the Mediterranean, your figs will produce two harvests. However, in cooler regions, figs crop just once a year. By late summer to autumn the fruit should be soft and ripe – the darkening colour of the fruit indicates its ripeness.

HOME REMEDIES

It is said that steeping 2 or 3 figs in milk overnight and then eating them in the morning can help improve sexual vigour – though this could also make you gain weight, so be cautious when trying this fig-and-milk combo. Eaten raw, figs can lower blood pressure, provide a calming effect on the body and treat piles and constipation. A tea made by infusing a couple of fig leaves in boiling water can help lower cholesterol levels. Dried leaves can make a tea that helps reduce blood sugar levels.

CULINARY USES

Fig syrup is delicious served on desserts and is a great option for flavouring cocktails. Fresh figs can be preserved in brandy and spices, poached in spiced wine and used to make a delicious sticky jam. Fig leaves can be used in cooking too – add them to your rice while cooking for a creamy result.

ALPINE STRAWBERRY

(FRAGARIA VESCA)

Once you've grown your own strawberries, you'll never look back. To my mind, they're like homegrown tomatoes: their flavour and texture is incomparable to shop-bought alternatives and they're much cheaper too. You simply can't beat eating a freshly-picked strawberry. At least, that's what I thought until I tried growing alpine strawberries this year.

Why hasn't everyone caught on about these delicious little rubies? They're tasty, pretty, contain more vitamins than hybridized cultivars and are surprisingly useful in the medicine cabinet as well as in the kitchen. True, the size of the fruit is significantly smaller when compared with cultivated varieties, so you'll need half a dozen or so plants to have a meaningful crop, but trust me, it's worth squeezing them into your plot.

Slugs and snails are pretty partial to strawberries, and alpine strawberries are no exception. The answer is to raise them off the ground. Last year I visited a local pick-your-own fruit farm, which now grows most of its strawberries using the "table-top" method. Just as it sounds, plants are grown in grow bags placed on A-frames, which makes it easier to water the plants and pick the fruit, as well as preventing soil-borne diseases and unwanted visitors from decimating the crop. If the experts are doing it, who am I to argue?

If your garden is on the small side or you only have a balcony, it makes sense to make the most of "empty" vertical spaces. Hanging baskets will do the job, and they are an inexpensive option. I've seen strawberries grown in colourful colanders, which are an ideal alternative to regular hanging baskets, especially if you're partial to a bit of upcyling. For my garden, I was really pleased to find a rusted iron sphere in a reclamation centre; it was a great size and easy to transform into a hanging basket.

To make a hanging basket sphere for your strawberries, you will need: a sphere or something similar (eBay and Etsy are good places to look, and modern ones are available in garden centres, too), hessian, a needle, string, a pen knife, compost and strawberry plants.

Line the bottom half of the sphere with a double layer of hessian, using a needle and string to secure the hessian to the sphere wherever possible. (By only half-filling the sphere, you will still be able to see the shape of the structure when the strawberries mature.) Fill the hessian-lined portion of the "basket" with compost. Using a pen knife, cut a series of slits in the hessian lining at 25cm (10in) intervals around the sphere. Plant strawberry plants in the slits around the sides of the "basket" and plant more of them in the surface of the compost.

GROW ⊕ H 0.1-0.5M; W 0.5-1M

For my garden, I went for the woodland alpine variety *Fragaria vesca* because it's happy to produce fruit in a bit of shade, which is very useful in my plot. While you can grow this plant from seed, I think buying young plants is a better bet, allowing you to save space on the windowsill or in your glasshouse for easier crops. When planting, ensure that the crown of the plant is level with the soil – too deep and the plant is likely to rot; too shallow and it'll dry out and die.

HANGING BASKET PROJECT

Other types of alpine strawberries you could try include:

- 'Mignonette' for an abundant crop.

- 'Alexandria' for very little maintenance – it doesn't even send out runners.

- 'Mara des Bois', a sophisticated French relative that combines both cultivated (size) and woodland (flavour) characteristics. Apparently, chefs love it and it's on my list for next season…

- *F. moschata,* for its distinctive flavour (imagine the love child from a tryst between a strawberry and a pineapple).

CARE

Water regularly and feed weekly when the plants are in flower if you're growing in hanging baskets. Remove runners to prevent them weakening the plant – you can plant these runners as you would the young plants. When the main plant has matured, divide in early spring just as the new growth appears.

PESTS & DISEASES

Watch out for determined slugs and snails. Mildew can be a problem, too. If your plants are affected by mildew, remove the leaves or the entire plant to prevent it becoming an issue.

HARVEST & STORAGE

Some people say that alpine strawberries are misleadingly called "everbearing", but I think a plant that produces fruit from spring until the first frosts has earned that accolade. The strawberries are borne on taller stems than cultivated varieties, so in a hanging basket, and upside down, they dangle

You can grow this alpine strawberry on your windowsill or in any sunny indoor spot. Just pop the plants outside over winter because they need to feel the cold in order to flower the following summer. By late winter, they should be ready to come back inside, where temperatures shouldn't exceed 16°C (60°F). It's fun growing strawberries indoors because you have to make like a bee and pollinate the flowers. A soft paint brush, gently stroked over the central yellow part of the flowers, will do the job.

rather gorgeously, like gaudy earrings, which makes the fruit easy to spot. Pick when the strawberries are absolutely ripe to get the most intense flavour and use fresh – they don't store well.

HOME REMEDIES

You can boil strawberry leaves in water to make a gargle for sore throats or use them to make a tea to calm an upset tummy.

I was particularly excited to discover that you can make both a toothpaste and toothpowder from strawberries. For strawberry toothpaste, mix mashed fresh strawberries with bicarbonate of soda. Make it as you need – a couple of strawberries to a dash of bicarb (mine turned black in the fridge, though kept separately, the mashed strawberries kept colour). For strawberry toothpowder, dry the leaves (overnight is sufficient) and then blitz them in the food processor or blender. Surely my son can't complain about brushing his teeth if the toothpaste is made from strawberries?

CULINARY USES

In addition to being a great source of vitamin C, tea made from the leaves can be drunk as an alternative to green tea if you're cutting out caffeine. And I love the idea that you could even use a dried alpine strawberry as a sweetener for your tea.

If you've treated yourself to several plants, you must have a go at making a strawberry compote. Use equal quantities of sugar and fruit, a few squeezes of lemon juice and a knob of butter to disperse any scum that forms when the liquid is boiling. I've read, though haven't tried yet, that adding a few juniper berries to the mixture introduces a spicy note.

The Swedes love alpine strawberries (they're called *smultron* in Swedish), foraging for them in forests and growing them in their gardens. They use them to flavour ice cream, cakes, mineral water and lozenges.

WILDLIFE BROWNIE POINTS

Alpine strawberries are the snack of choice for the larvae of the grizzled skipper butterfly – a demure chocolate-brown and white butterfly that sadly is becoming increasingly rare.

CAUTION

An allergic reaction to contact with strawberry leaves in the form of a rash is extremely rare but not unheard of. Avoid eating the fruit if you have a known or suspected allergy to strawberries.

DWARF DAMSON

(PRUNUS INSITITIA 'FARLEIGH DAMSON')

The dwarf greengage plum variety I found for my garden was discovered nearly 200 years ago in Farleigh, a village in Kent, England. Sadly, it needs another partner for pollination, so requires double the space of the self-fertile dwarf damson, Dwarf Patio Damson 'Merryweather'. The good news is that growing two trees instead of one means lots more fruit: hello, damson gin, damson vodka and all manner of other tasty treats.

GROW ⬥ H 2-2.5M; W 0.05M

This dwarf variety is grafted onto a rootstock that will only reach 2.5m (8¼ft) in height, yet still produces plenty of fruit in early autumn. Plant it in a good-sized (60cm/2ft) container with plenty of well-rotted organic matter incorporated into the compost. Choose a sunny, sheltered spot.

CARE

Keep well-watered during warm weather and feed once a year with a seaweed liquid feed. Think about repotting after 5 or 6 years, increasing the size of the container by about 10cm (4in). Alternatively, you can prune the roots to curtail the tree's growth: during the dormant winter months, shave off some of the roots if the root ball is very congested and repot with fresh compost.

PESTS & DISEASES

Sawfly, leaf curl and aphids.

HARVEST & STORAGE

Pick the fruit in late summer or early autumn. Fruits can be frozen or used fresh.

HOME REMEDIES

The fresh fruit provide a good source of fibre, which aids the digestive system and can help reduce cholesterol. Damsons are also rich in magnesium, which means they can aid sleep.

CULINARY USES

Despite their tartness when tasted raw, damsons contain more sugar than plums. Their sugar content means that they are great for making preserves and don't need too much in the way of an added sweetener. Damsons can be turned into a delicious "cheese" (think membrillo instead of goat's cheese) and a sensational flavoured vodka. To make damson vodka, use 500g (18oz) of damsons per litre (1¾ pints) of vodka. If you like a bit more of an involved process, damson wine is meant to taste pretty good, too, though I've not been lucky enough to try it yet. It requires a bit more in the way of specialized ingredients; the recipes I've seen call for pectic enzyme, Campden tablets, wine yeast and yeast nutrient.

SLOE

(PRUNUS SPINOSA)

I'm pretty sure my younger self would have been delighted to be told I would one day have the opportunity to write this book. When I was a child, my parents would take my sister and I on countless wet and windy autumn walks in search of sloes. Naturally, at the time, I didn't appreciate that the reward for these forays was delicious flavoured gin. Apparently, I complained constantly as we trudged up and down hedgerows in search of the fruit, and it didn't help that we'd get pricked by the thorny branches in thanks for our efforts.

Mum and Dad's sloe gin was, and still is, legendary. I'm determined to keep the family tradition alive, which means in recent years my poor son has had to suffer the same foraging fate I endured as a child. Well, he did until I decided I'd like to grow a sloe (also known as a blackthorn) as part of the hedge in my front garden. However, reading up about this wild native, I've realized it will actually take several years before my sloe can provide me with enough fruit for a litre or two of gin. Poor boy, it turns out my son hasn't escaped this tradition just yet.

GROW ⬭ H 2.5-4M; W 2.5-4M

Though the sloe isn't fussy about soil (it grows happily on scrubland), it's best grown in the ground rather than in a container. That doesn't mean it has to become a large specimen; annual pruning can maintain this shrub at a height of 1.8m (6ft). Choose a sunny spot to encourage plenty of fruit and water regularly in the first year.

CARE

Add a layer of mulch around the base of young bushes in spring to help them become established. Prune in summer, especially if you're trying to restrict the shrub's height. Water regularly throughout the growing season.

PESTS & DISEASES

Birds.

HARVEST & STORAGE

Wait until a couple of frosts have passed before picking the fruit. The frosts soften the skins of the fruit, which helps the gin to seep in and absorb the flavour more readily.

HOME REMEDIES

A tea made from leaves and dried sloes will settle stomach complaints and help to combat colds and flu. Gargle with fresh sloe juice or a tea made from the dried fruit to relieve mouth ulcers and sore throats.

CULINARY USES

To make sloe gin, you'll need about 450g (1lb) sloes and 1 litre (1¾ pints) gin. Prick the sloe skins all over and then place them in a sterilized jar. At this point, you can add some sugar (about 225g/8oz, or to taste), although I think it's best to sweeten the liquor with sugar syrup, adding a little at a time, to taste, after the sloes have flavoured the gin. Either way, pour over the gin, seal the jar and shake well. Store in a cool cupboard, shaking every few days for about 2 months. To strain, pour through a sieve or muslin cloth. You can drink the sloe gin the same year you make it, but I find keeping it until the following Christmas improves the flavour.

Like plums, sloes make delicious wine, jelly, syrup and jam. In France, the unripe fruits are pickled like olives.

WILD AND FREE

Don't despair if you haven't space in your garden for a sloe bush or two; they grow very happily in the wild. If you're not sure what to look for, keep an eye out for bushes with white flowers on bare stems in early spring and make a mental note about the location so you can return in the autumn to pick the fruit for free.

RHUBARB

(RHEUM × HYBRIDUM)

My parents grew rhubarb at the bottom of the garden of my childhood home. Every spring, my sister and I used to pick fresh stems and eat them raw, dipping them in a little bag of sugar for every mouthful. It was delicious, though I think we might have ended up with stomach ache more often than not, given the amount we ate. Rhubarb will be a great addition to any garden because it can cope in semi-shade and provides some structure, thanks to its architectural shape, beautiful red stems and large lush leaves.

GROW ◶ H 0.5-1M; W 0.5-1M

While you can plant rhubarb at any time of year, autumn or early spring is best. Whether planting in a large container or in the ground, make sure the compost has plenty of well-rotted manure added to it. When planting, make sure the growing point of the crown is level or just below the surface of the soil.

Maincrop rhubarb (best-loved for their tangy, tart flavour) will produce edible stems from early spring to the end of summer. If you'd like to harvest rhubarb earlier than that, you need to "force" rhubarb, which produces sweet, tender, pretty pink stems as early as the beginning of the year, until early spring. While commercial forcing is done with controlled light and growing conditions, you can do it at home by covering the crown of the plant with a layer of straw in the new year and putting a bucket or terracotta pot over the plant to exclude the light. The forced rhubarb will be ready to harvest about two months later. If you force rhubarb, let the plant rest every couple of years as forcing can weaken it.

CARE

Keep plants healthy by lifting and dividing the crowns after a few years – the best time to do this is from early spring to early summer. Let the leaves die back over the autumn then remove them, exposing the growing point to the cold.

While the leaves are poisonous, they can be composted as the oxalic acid breaks down during the process.

PESTS & DISEASES

Crown rot.

HARVEST & STORAGE

Wait until the second season before picking the rhubarb, and then only pick a few stems. To prevent the crown rotting, twist and pull stems (rather than cutting them) so they're removed at the crown.

HOME REMEDIES

Powdered rhubarb (made from the dried root and stem) can be used to make a tincture that helps with digestion and stomach cramps.

CULINARY USES

Over and above the ubiquitous (and tasty) rhubarb crumble, try making jelly, curd and chutney. Rhubarb can also be used to flavour vodka or to make a syrup for cocktails.

CURRANTS

(RIBES SPP.)

Currants are the ideal fruit for containers, whether that's on a roof terrace, a balcony, the doorstep or in your backyard. The bushes produce a meaningful bounty and, given you can grow black, red, white and pink berries, you've got a flash of colour to feast your eyes on when the jewel-like fruits are ready to harvest. I grow my currants in individual pots, grouping them together – a cornucopia of currants, if you will.

GROW ⊖ H: 1-1.5M; W 1-1.5M

For the best berries, plant your bushes in well-drained soil that retains moisture (either add lots of organic material or mulch at planting time) and provide them with plenty of sun. Like other cane fruit, you can buy bare-root plants during the dormant season. To plant, make sure the planting hole is twice as big as the roots and gently spread them out before covering with soil. Take note: blackcurrants are planted 5cm (2in) lower than they were in their original pot, while redcurrants and white currants are planted at the same level. You'll see what I mean when you look at the stem and see lighter and darker wood. The reason for this is that blackcurrants are multi-stemmed and send out shoots from the base, while redcurrants and white currants form a bush on a single stem. Once planted, prune the shoots back to about 2.5cm (1in) as this will stimulate young shoots. However, if you've bought your currants in a container, don't hard prune and feel free to plant at any time of year.

CARE

Prune when the growing season is over, from late autumn to late winter. As currant bushes produce their fruit on younger stems, concentrate on removing the older ones to improve the shape of the bush and encourage new growth. Make sure plants have enough space for air to circulate to help prevent pests and diseases.

PESTS & DISEASES

Birds, gooseberry mildew, big bud mites and gall midges.

HARVEST & STORAGE

Depending on the variety you grow, either pick an entire string of berries or pick the berries individually if the top ones are riper than those at the bottom of the string. If you're not able to eat all the berries the same day, pop them into the freezer.

HOME REMEDIES

Blackcurrant juice helps soothe sore throats and can be used to make lozenges. The leaves can be infused into an aromatic tea that cleanses the system, or crushed to help relieve insect bites.

CULINARY USES

Currants have high levels of pectin, which means they are great for making into jams and jellies. I love to use the frozen currants as colourful ice cubes. To make a cordial, put 500g (1lb 2oz) currants and 300ml (10fl oz) water in a heatproof glass bowl. Set the bowl over a bain marie and heat for about an hour (squishing the fruit from time to time to help release the juice). Strain into a bowl, weight it, then transfer to a saucepan and add 250g (9oz) sugar (or a few stevia leaves) for every 600ml (1 pint) juice. (The amount of sugar can be changed, depending on your taste.) Gently heat until the sugar has dissolved (or the stevia imparted its flavour). Pour into sterilized bottles and store in the refrigerator. It will keep for up to 1 month.

RASPBERRY

(RUBUS IDAEUS)

Raspberries don't need as much room as you might think. I have a friend who grows them at the back of a narrow border, allowing them to do their thing while she grows more showy herbs and later summer flowers like dahlias in front of them. If space in the ground is out of the question, there are dwarf varieties that can be grown in a container and will produce a meaningful harvest for you to enjoy.

I tried growing 'Ruby Beauty' (*Rubus idaeus*) and was delighted with the tasty berries that appeared in early summer and throughout the summer. There are also varieties you can grow in hanging baskets. When selecting plants, it's worth checking when they fruit; you could choose both summer- and autumn-bearing raspberries to provide you with a longer season of fruit.

GROW ◑ H 0.5-1.5M; W 0.5-1M

Make sure the soil is free-draining – raspberries don't appreciate wet feet – and is full of rich, well-rotted organic matter. A bit of shade is fine but these plants are best suited to sunny spots. While you don't need to worry about supporting the compact dwarf varieties (they only reach 1m/3¼ft in height), if the stems are bearing a lot of fruit, you might want to pop in a bamboo cane or two.

CARE

Mulch raspberries in the winter and keep the area free of weeds. Prune out the canes that produce fruit over the summer, cutting them back to the base of the plant. Leave the remaining canes in place for next year's fruit.

PESTS & DISEASES

Raspberry beetle.

HARVEST & STORAGE

Pick fruit when ripe and use fresh or freeze. Leaves should be harvested in spring before the flowers appear and then dried.

HOME REMEDIES

A raspberry leaf infusion can be gargled for sore throats and mouths or used to wash wounds and ulcers. Raspberry leaf tea is reputed to strengthen the muscles of the uterus and ease labour.

To make a tincture that helps relieve period pain, wash and pat dry 2 cups fresh raspberry leaves and pack into a sterilized jar. Pour in just enough boiling water to cover the leaves then top up the jar with vodka. Leave in a cool, dark place for up to 6 weeks, shaking every week. Strain and transfer the tincture to a clean, sterilized jar. Label and use as required.

CULINARY USES

In addition to jams and jellies, you can use the fruit to flavour vinegar. To make spiced raspberries, boil the fruit in a mixture of vinegar, sugar, cinnamon, cloves and mace for 45 minutes, then strain and store in a sterilized jar.

CHILEAN GUAVA

(UGNI MOLINAE)

I bought this shrub several years ago for a book I was writing about container-grown fruit and vegetables. It's been in my garden ever since and it's more than earned its keep. Quite apart from the annual bountiful crop of lipstick-red berries that taste a bit like blueberries with a floral note, this shrub is evergreen and I use it like a box ball to add a bit of interest and structure to the parts of my garden that look lacklustre in winter. It also looks very sweet with a small length of fairy lights threaded through its branches during the festive season.

I was surprised to read that William Lobb, the plant-hunting pioneer, introduced the Chilean guava to the UK in 1844. A jam made using the berries became a favourite of Queen Victoria, who had punnets of the fruit sent to her by train from Cornwall, where the shrub was grown.

GROW ⬭ H 2.5-3M; W 0.1-0.5M

Despite its name, I've found that the Chilean guava is a really hardy shrub, though I do have a walled city garden. My shrub endured 2017's harsh winter so I'm fairly confident it will cope in all but the coldest, wettest region without any winter protection.

CARE

Offer the plant some protection from cold wind if it's in a particularly exposed spot. Prune damaged and dead stems in spring.

PESTS & DISEASES

Generally free from pests and diseases. Watch out for peckish birds.

HARVEST & STORAGE

Pick berries in early winter – they make a great late-season treat. The berries can be eaten fresh, kept in the refrigerator or dried.

CULINARY USES

I've made muffins and jelly with the berries, and in Chile they're used to make pies. If you'd like to be a bit more creative, try cooking them with apples to make fruit leather. There are some delicious recipes on the internet that suggest steeping some lightly crushed berries and some orange peel in 1 litre (1¾ pints) of vodka or making a version of *murtado*, a traditional Chilean liqueur, that, as far as I can tell, is made by steeping the berries in brandy for a few weeks and then sweetening it with syrup.

BLUEBERRY, BILBERRY, HUCKLEBERRY & HONEYBERRY

(VACCINIUM SPP. AND LONICERA CAERULEA)

I remember discovering blueberries nearly 15 years ago, when I was working on *Gardeners' World* magazine and we featured an article about how to grow your own superfoods. I didn't need to be asked twice to grow delicious berries that are not just good for you, but super good for you. These days my son has two of "his own" pot-grown blueberry plants in the garden and the berries from these (as well as shop-bought ones, I have to confess) are a regular feature at our breakfast table. While blueberries were an obvious choice for this book, I've since found three other varieties of blue berries (two of which are related to the blueberry), so have included them too. What's not to like about growing a medley of blue fruit, some sweet, some sour and all ridiculously good for you?

GROW

They are all happy grown in the ground or in containers, they just need ericaceous soil, some sun and to be brought indoors out of direct sun in winter.

Blueberries are easy to grow and are hugely productive plants. I went for *Vaccinium* 'Blautropf' because it provides pretty teardrop-shaped berries from early summer until the first frosts. It's also a compact variety so is great for growing in pots under other acid-loving plants. 'Blautropf' grows to 60cm (2ft) tall and 40cm (16in) wide.

Bilberries (*Vaccinium myrtillus*) need at least two plants for cross-pollination, which is also helpful because the amount of berries produced on individual plants is relatively humble. Bilberries grow to 45cm (1½ft) tall. Huckleberries (*Vaccinium ovatum*) are a great choice if yours is a shady plot. Another bonus for this plant is that it's an evergreen. It grows to 1.4m (4¾ft) tall and 80cm (2¾ft) wide.

The final blue berry I grow isn't actually related to blueberries. The honeyberry (*Lonicera caerulea*) is a cousin of honeysuckle and it has a shrub form and produces delicious and edible fruit. I plumped for 'Blue Moon' because it is compact, which is useful in tight spots, and its berries are bigger than usual. You'll need another plant for cross-pollination – I went for 'Blue Sea', which produces plenty of fruits. They grow to 80cm (2¾ft) tall and 1m (3¼ft) wide.

CARE

Blueberries are easy to grow. Given the right care (pruning out dead and diseased canes, as well as a couple of older canes each year, once the plant is 2–3 years old), these plants will produce berries for years to come. Water regularly, with rainwater if at all possible, as tap water will alter the pH of the ericaceous soil. Bilberries don't require too much in the way of TLC, just a prune after they've produced the berries and a mulch in spring.

Huckleberries are slow-growing plants, so only require pruning to keep them healthy. Wait for summer to prune your honeyberry – simply remove old growing stems to encourage new growth.

HARVEST & STORAGE
- Blueberry: midsummer–early autumn
- Bilberry: midsummer–late summer
- Huckleberry: late summer–early autumn
- Honeyberry: early summer

PESTS & DISEASES

Birds (all) and powdery mildew (blueberry).

HOME REMEDIES

The blue berries of these plants are all rich in antioxidants. Blueberry juice is used to help coughs and is said to prevent wrinkles, age spots and acne. It's also a mood enhancer, has anti-inflammatory properties, encourages hair growth (if mixed with olive oil and applied to hair roots), maintains eye health, helps digestion and lowers cholesterol.

Bilberries, which contain four times more anthocyanin (the plant pigment that makes them blue) than blueberries, have been used to help all manner of illnesses, from diabetes to eye conditions. Eating the raw berries can reduce gum inflammation and help with varicose veins and haemorrhoids because they strengthen the walls of blood vessels. A tea made from the fruit and leaves can help reduce blood sugar levels.

Huckleberry leaves have antiseptic qualities. A decoction of the leaves can be helpful with diabetes. Tea made from the leaves and dried fruit is a great source of vitamin C and boosts immunity. Honeyberries don't appear to have any recognized medicinal uses, though I've read that research is being undertaken to determine their anti-inflammatory properties.

CULINARY USES

Blueberry juice can be used to make a syrup to flavour desserts. All the berries can be used to make jam/jelly, fill tarts and pies or just eaten raw.

WASABI

(WASABIA JAPONICA)

I've grown wasabi in a medium-sized container for several years. It's easier than you might think, given the plant's exotic origins, but you'll need to be patient as it takes a couple of years to mature. However, gram for gram, wasabi is considered to be the most expensive vegetable in the world, so when you do get to harvest your first crop, trust me, it feels pretty great. One of the early stars of the spring garden, wasabi puts on lots of glossy green heart-shaped leaves that provide a much-needed splash of colour when most of the garden is only just starting to come to life. Leaves die back in summer sunshine and over winter, but during spring and autumn you can enjoy the vibrant display. This is also a useful plant if you're growing in a small space because it's happy to lurk in a shady corner where many other plants might struggle. In fact, one year my wasabi positively thrived, forgotten and tucked behind another plant.

GROW ⬬ H 0.1-0.5M; W 0.1-0.5M

You can raise wasabi from seed, though it can be difficult to get hold of viable stock. Even then, it can be a bit of a challenge to get the seeds going so, I recommend buying a young plant. While it's the more expensive option, it is worth the investment as it gets you off to a better start.

CARE

This perennial is native to the mountain regions of Japan, where it can be found thriving next to streams and rivers, which explains why my plant felt so at home in its cool, shady and moist position. If you're growing it in a container, add some perlite or gravel at the base of the pot to help with drainage as the plant won't do well in waterlogged soil. Great news: if you don't have a lot of – or any – outdoor space, you can grow wasabi indoors. Keep it out of direct sunlight and water regularly.

PESTS & DISEASES

Watch out for slugs and snails, which can ruin the beautifully shaped foliage in the blink of an eye.

HARVEST & STORAGE

A member of the *Brassicaceae* family, otherwise known as the mustard family, wasabi looks very similar to its relative horseradish, albeit lime green rather than creamy white. The wasabi's leaves and flowers are edible (they taste delicious pickled with sugar and salt), so this great plant will definitely earn its space in your garden while its roots mature. It can take 18–24 months for the swollen root of the wasabi to develop its distinctive flavour. To harvest, lift the plant out of the soil and remove any small offshoots at the base of the plant. Pot-up the offshoots and grow on to make your next crop.

HOME REMEDIES

An anti-inflammatory, wasabi is good for arthritis and pain in joints. It's great for clearing sinus passages and it is believed to prevent bacteria from clinging to teeth, so reduces chances of tooth decay.

CULINARY USES

You really need to grow your own wasabi to experience its true flavour. It's nothing like the wasabi you get with restaurant sushi, which is a combination of horseradish, mustard, sugar and green dye. The root is best used fresh – it loses its potency after 15 minutes, so grate as required. Remember, a little wasabi goes a long way!

THE LITTLE BLACK BOOK
OF PESTS & DISEASES

I'm bound to say that prevention is always better than cure when it comes to coping with pests and diseases. A vigorous healthy plant will be less susceptible to nasties than a weak one. Always keep your tools clean and don't let a lot of debris build up around plants, especially in a small garden where ventilation around plants might be poor. A garden filled with wildlife and beneficial insects, such as ladybirds and lacewings, will help control pests and disease, too.

If you are unlucky and your plants are affected by pests or diseases, always choose an organic non-chemical solution. Not only is this option better for the environment, it's better for you too: don't forget you're going to be using your crops in your cooking and to make home remedies.

PESTS

APHIDS

Aphids are tiny pear-shaped insects, such as blackfly and greenfly, that suck plant juices and leave behind a sticky residue that attracts honeydew fungus – double trouble! Encourage natural predators, such as lacewing, hoverfly larvae and ladybirds. If it's a bad infestation, spray with a strong jet of water, being careful not to damage the plant.

BEETLES (MINT BEETLE & ROSEMARY BEETLE)

Mint beetles and rosemary beetles are gorgeous to look at, but these metallic beauties can be a pain if you don't like to share your harvests. However, I think it's best to live and let live, especially as the herbs these two types of beetle attack are relatively robust and likely to produce plenty of foliage.

BIG BUD MITE

Taking up residence inside buds, big bud mites eventually make buds dry up and stunt growth. Pick off infected buds or, if the infestation is bad, replace the plant with healthy stock.

BIRDS

Birds can be a tricky problem when growing crops. Essentially, you're in a race to protect your fruit bushes and trees before the birds strip them of their delicious bounty. Netting is the best material to use.

CAPSID BUG

Telltale signs you have these visitors are small holes near buds. Capsid-bug damage can prevent buds developing. Keep the area surrounding your plant free from debris so that the bugs can't overwinter.

CARROT FLY

The larvae of the carrot fly can cause scar rings near the roots of carrots and holes in the vegetables that run throughout the crop and make them inedible. Sow carrot seed sparingly to avoid the need to thin out seedlings and cover plants with a barrier of horticultural fleece.

FLEA BEETLE

An infestation of flea beetles can make leaves look like doilies. The tiny holes made by the beetles damage the leaves and make them susceptible to diseases. To prevent flea beetles, rake and moisten the soil surrounding the plant; the adult beetles don't like to lay eggs on damp soil and the larvae don't like to be disturbed.

GALL MIDGE

The hungry larvae of the gall midge will attack new leaf growth, which will ultimately stunt a plant's growth. Unless you're unlucky enough to have a terrible infestation, you don't need to worry about this pest as it doesn't affect cropping. Remove infected material if you're concerned.

LEAF-HOPPERS

The leaf-hopper is another juice-sucking pest. These bad guys can stunt a plant's growth and cause leaves to curl or appear burned. Try spraying affected plants with a strong jet of water. If the problem is persistent, call in the big guns: parasitic wasps, which are a biological control, can be bought online.

LEAF MINER

Leaf miners – the hungry larvae of flies, moths, sawflies and beetles – burrow into leaves and munch their way around, leaving unsightly wiggly or straight white lines on the surface. Remove affected leaves and cover plants with horticultural fleece.

MEALYBUGS

Mealybugs can easily be mistaken for white fluff on leaves; this white substance is actually the tiny bug covered in wax that has a dusty texture. The best way to control these sap-sucking pests is to spray them with water or neem oil (an organic pest control). For glasshouse plants, remove mealy bugs with a cotton bud soaked in alcohol. Failing that, try introducing parasitic wasps to control this pest.

MICE & VOLES

Given that mice and voles can eat their way through bulbs, fruit and seeds, most gardeners want to do away with these furry creatures. The best solution is to introduce a barrier around the object of their affection. You can use wire mesh to protect bulbs or netting to cover fruit.

SAWFLY

You'd be forgiven for mistaking sawfly larvae for caterpillars because, well, they look like caterpillars. However, sawfly larvae have more pairs of legs than caterpillars – seven compared to three. Sawflies are closely related to bees, wasps and ants. They can have three lots of feeding young in one season, and they can strip foliage from plants very quickly. Remove the larvae by hand and squash underfoot. Attract beneficial insects to your garden to keep this pest under control.

SCALE INSECT

Smooth brown or white bumps on a plant's stems or leaves are an indication of a scale-insect attack. Yellowing leaves are another sign. Pick off scale insects by hand or use a cotton bud soaked in alcohol to remove them. Prune infected areas. Ladybirds and parasitic wasps will hoover up this pest.

BAY SUCKER

I'm sad to say that my bay trees always seem to end up afflicted with this small sap-sucking insect. It's easy to spot in the summer, as leaves discolour, curl at the edges and eventually sections turn brown. So long as the plant isn't too small, it's not the end of the world and is more a question of being unsightly rather than damaging. Keep on top of it by picking off infected leaves and burn them.

SLUGS AND SNAILS

Recent research has shown that homemade methods for controlling slugs and snails don't work. So, fill your wormery (see page 14) with the egg shells, beer, coffee grounds and orange peel that you might have used to try to deter these pests and opt for organic pet-friendly slug pellets instead. I also recommend a midnight forage around your garden to collect slugs and snails by hand, then simply discard them in any way that still allows you to sleep at night.

SPIDER MITES

These critters turn healthy leaves a bronze colour and create a stippled effect that eventually kills the leaf. Attract beneficial insects such as the predatory mite Neoseiulus californicus, which you can buy online, to control this pest and keep plants cool and moist.

RASPBERRY BEETLE

A troublesome pest that, in its larvae form eats the fruit, and in its adult form devours buds and blossom. Disturb the soil around the base of the plant in spring to bring the larvae to the surface, where they can be picked off and squashed, or left for the birds. You can also buy traps to put out a month before buds appear.

VINE WEEVIL

Vine weevils are really annoying pests that can wreak havoc by attacking the roots and root crown of your plants. The larvae do most of the damage. Keep the area surrounding the plant tidy so that the larvae can't hide or overwinter in debris and try placing a cloth around the base of the plant at night and shaking it to disturb the weevils. Discard the weevils in a bucket of soapy water.

WHITEFLY

These small white insects more often strike in glasshouses than outdoors. They suck a plant's juices, which can cause the plant to wilt, and they also leave behind a sticky residue that attracts honeydew fungus. Remove infested plant matter and destroy it. Hang up sticky traps to control this pest. If the infestation is very bad, try to attract ladybirds with pollen-rich plants such as fennel, caraway, angelica and marigolds, to name but a few that I've included in this book, or introduce parasitic wasps.

WEBBER MOTH CATERPILLARS

Dichomeris marginella creates a web within which larvae hang out and feed on the needles towards the end of the summer. Hard to control organically, so your best bet is to cut off and destroy infected branches.

DISEASES

ARBUTUS LEAF SPOT

This disease causes unsightly spots to appear on leaves and twigs, and ultimately they might die. Remove infected plant material.

DOWNY MILDEW

Check for discoloured areas on the tops of leaves and for white mould on the undersides of leaves. Remove and destroy infected plant material and in warm weather avoid watering late in the evening.

GOOSEBERRY MILDEW

This is another white mould-like disease that can damage leaves and fruits. Allow plenty of air to circulate around the plant and remove damaged plant material.

GREY MOULD

Looking just like classic mould, grey mould can appear if plants are damaged or if the conditions are very humid. If possible, reduce humidity and don't feed plants with too much nitrogen-rich fertilizer as this can encourage soft leaf growth. Remove and destroy affected plant material.

HONEY FUNGUS

This fungus is hard to spot; it spreads underground, killing roots, and often the first time you're aware of it is when the plant dies. Honey fungus can do a lot of damage and it's really hard to treat, so dig up and destroy infected plants and remove the soil around it. Try using a physical barrier like butyl rubber pond lining to prevent the fungus from spreading.

LEAF CURL

There's no mistaking a plant infected with this disease as its leaves literally crumple and curl up. The best way to try to avoid leaf curl is to use a plastic sheet to protect plants from rain between early winter and late spring. However, you need to allow pollinating insects access to the plant, so look online for suggestions for how to erect plastic sheeting.

LEAF SPOT

If you find dots of dead material on a leaf, remove the infected plant material or prune back infected stems. Make sure there's plenty of ventilation around the plant.

MOSAIC VIRUS

This plant virus causes leaves to have a mottled yellow appearance with light green spots that seem raised. Unfortunately, once a plant is infected it needs to be destroyed and replaced.

POWDERY MILDEW

Look out for powdery white growth on leaves. To avoid powdery mildew, water plants regularly and provide space for good air circulation.

SOFT ROT

This is a bacterial rather than fungal disease which lives in the soil. The smell from the rotting plant is more pungent than with fungal rots. Remove infected plants and destroy.

RHIZOME ROT

Watch out for drying leaves and stunted roots. Don't let soil remain waterlogged and remove any diseased plants.

RUST

Rust is an unsightly disease. Its calling card is pustules on leaves that can be a variety of colours, including orange, yellow, brown, black and white. Though rust is unattractive, it's largely OK to pick off infected leaves and not worry too much about it.

TWIG BLIGHT

Twig blight causes leaves to turn brown and die and stems to present with brown lesions. Remove and destroy all infected plant material.

GENERIC ROT

If you experience crown, rhizome or root rot, remove the infected leaves and destroy badly infected plants.

INDEX

ACKNOWLEDGEMENTS

Huge thanks to Celia at Suttons, the Hetty's Herb team, Stephen at Victoriana Nursery, Sonia at Thompson & Morgan, Fran at Rabbit Attack PR/Lubera, Vicky at Lime Cross Nursery, David Smale at English Saffron and Mark & Katy at Hortus Loci; Nicola Rathbone at Bristol Botanic Garden for all your help and advice. Mark Diacono, Alys Fowler and lastly, but by no means least, Jekka McVicar – you're all so busy and brilliant and yet you found the time to share your wisdom with me… thank you.

Thank you so much, Sophie – confirming our book deal on International Women's Day was a huge moment, and one for which I shall be eternally grateful. Thank you for putting your faith in Tory and I to deliver your brilliant idea. Thank you to Nicky Collings and Aaron Blecha for making it look gorgeous, to Clare, for your fantastic subbing and to all the team at Kyle Books.

Mum, Dad, Ava, George and Paul – thank you for pitching in and helping so that Tory and I could get on with the job - where would we be without you all. Thanks Polly and Sarah for being such game and gorgeous models, Geeta, for introducing me to Danny and Naomi for making me take the leap to start remodelling the garden.

Darling little Hal, you're the inspiration for it all and I hope you'll be proud of your mum's books some day, even though you really want grass and a trampoline in our garden. And Tory, thank you thank you thank you for your beautiful pictures – who knew working on a book project could be so relaxed and so much fun. Whispering in the garden at 4.30am during that glorious hot summer will stay in my memory forever.

BIBLIOGRAPHY

Tonics & Teas by Rachel de Thample (Kyle Books, 2017)

Tonic by Tanita de Ruijt (Hardie Grant, 2017)

Backyard Foraging by Ellen Zachos (Storey Publishing, 2013)

Composting with Worms by George Pilkington
  (Eco-Logic Books, 2005)

The Wild and Weedy Apothecary by Doreen Shababy
  (Llewellyn Publications, 2016)

Alchemy of Herbs by Rosalee de la Foret (Hay House, 2017)

The Gardener's Companion to Medicinal Plants
  by Monique Simmonds, Melanie-Jayne Howes & Jason Irving
  (Frances Lincoln, 2016)

The Handmade Apothecary by Victoria Chown & Kim Walker
  (Kyle Books, 2017)

The Herball's Guide to Botanical Drinks by Michael Isted
  (Jacqui Small, 2018)

The Illustrated Herb Book by John Lust (Dover Publications, 2014)

Llewellyn's 2018 Herbal Almanac (Llewellyn Publications)

RESOURCES

Suttons Seeds, Tel: 0333 4002899 www.suttons.co.uk

Hetty's Herbs and Plants Tel: 01775 663 790 www.hettysherbs.co.uk

Psychopomp Microdistillery tel 07511934675
  www.microdistillery.co.uk

Thompson & Morgan Tel: 01473 695378 www.thompson-morgan.com

English Saffron - englishsaffron.co.uk

Lubera AG, Tel: +41 (0)81 740 58 33 www.lubera.com

Lime Cross Nursery, Tel: 01323 833 229 www.limecross.co.uk

Victoriana Nursery Gardens, Tel: 01233 740529
  www.victoriananursery.co.uk

Jekka's Herb Farm Tel: 01454 418878. www.jekkasherbfarm.com

Surreal Succulents. www.surrealsucculents.co.uk

Hortus Loci Ltd, Tel: 0118 9326 495. www.hortusloci.co.uk

Wildegoose Nursery, T: 01584 841890. www.wildegoosenursery.co.uk

University of Bristol Botanic GardeTel: 0117 928 9000
  www.bristol.ac.uk/botanic-garden/